NORWEGIAN
KNITTING DESIGNS

A COLLECTION FROM SOME OF
NORWAY'S LEADING KNITTING
DESIGNERS

EDITOR:
MARGARETHA FINSETH

Search Press

This edition published in Great Britain in 2019
Search Press Ltd.,
Wellwood, North Farm Road, Tunbridge Wells,
Kent, United Kingdom, TN2 3DR

Previously published in Great Britain in 2011 (reprinted 2012)
by Search Press.
Previously published in the USA in 2002 by Unicorn Books and Crafts,
Inc. as *Norsk Strikkedesign: A Collection from Norway's Foremost
Knitting Designers.*
Originally published in Norway in 1999 by N.W. Damm & Søn AS, as
Norsk strikkedesign: Norges fremste strikkedesignere.

Translation: Carol Huebscher Rhoades
Patterns and Charts: Gro Sandvik
Technical Editor: Elisabeth Zaborowski
Photography: Ragnar Hartvig
Makeup, Hair and Styling: Per Ragnar Karlsen
Outdoor Photos: Bård Løken, pages 6, 34, 54, 84, 94 and
front and back covers
Graphic Design: Ashley Booth Design AS
Reproduction: Larvik Litho AS
Printed in China by 1010 Printing International Ltd.

The translation of this book has been financial supported by MUNIN –
Marketing Unit for Norwegian International Non-fiction.

ISBN: 978-1-78221-712-1

The Publishers and author can accept no responsibility for any
consequences arising from the information, advice or instructions given
in this publication.

Readers are permitted to reproduce any of the items in this book for
their personal use, or for the purposes of selling for charity, free of
charge and without the prior permission of the Publishers. Any use of the
items for commercial purposes is not permitted without the prior
permission of the Publishers.

Thank you for lending materials for the photo styling:

Birkenstock	Ivan Grundahl
Blues	Kjell Thorheim
Eva Lie	NygaardsAnna
Hebbeding	Origo Design
Heimen	Stephanie Kelian

**Thank you to the following spinneries
who donated yarn for the book:**
ASA Gjestal Spinneri
Hillesvåg Ullvarefabrikk AS
Rauma Ullvarefabrikk AS (PT-Design)
SandnesGarn AS

CONTENTS

Participating designers:

FOREWORD

Our desire has been to present a colourful, lively and practical book which showcases the variety represented by some of our best knitwear designers. The designers featured in this book have influenced Norwegian hand- and commercial-knitting during the last twenty to thirty years. In these pages, you will meet designers who have worked for the Norwegian knitting industry, woollen mills and yarn spinneries, magazines and weekly papers. These are the creative women behind the lines of high-profile knitwear produced for the winter Olympics and World Cup ski competitions, as well as being designers of award-winning knitwear collections.

We are proud to be able to present a design book where the designers have had the opportunity to create unique, specially designed garments. Simple patterns for beginner knitters don't have a natural place in this collection; instead, we have collected over thirty practical designs which show how fantastic and lovely garments can grow from something as simple as needles and skeins of yarn. Hand-knitting allows an unbounded freedom to create a completely personal expression through colours, embellishments, structure and styling. Our intention is to demonstrate that freedom fully through this book. Most designers develop their distinctive persona and signature design style over time. When they go further and explore new creative expressions, their pieces then have the designer's special touch or 'fingerprint'. When you go through this book, you get a little glimpse of the different methods a designer uses to give form to new ideas. No designer works like another. From project to project, each designer draws different impressions and inspirations from quite varied sources. You would be surprised at how many objects can give birth to creativity – from an elegantly worked bridal crown or a postcard to nature's shifting light, grey stones and even rough logging roads. This becomes obvious when so many designers are presented side by side. It is striking to see how Norwegian designers are strong on ornamental techniques, cable patterns and, in particular, traditional motifs. Our knitting designers are the bearers of tradition as well as innovators: they present new and contemporary forms at an international level while continuing to develop a long and unbroken national knitting tradition.

We know that there have been knitted garments in Norway since the sixteenth century, possibly even from the fifteenth century. We have silk pieces from 1630 which tell us that knitting techniques were known in both Rogaland and Trøndelag, and it is clear that, between 1600 and 1700, knitting had spread to most parts of our country. Even in the early eighteenth century, cottage industries were producing hand-knitted garments for sale and were well established in certain areas. These then instigated the textile industry which, initially, produced machine-spun yarns for the home-based production of woven and knitted goods. This industry continued to expand until end of the nineteenth century.

In keeping with tradition, we have chosen to use classic Norwegian-spun wool yarns in this book, and our tradition-rich spinneries have contributed the yarns. Sheep are Norway's oldest domesticated animals and people originally kept sheep for their wool. Norwegians also have a long history of shepherding for meat, wool and skins. We have always been a careful people who know how to utilize resources to the utmost. Knitting has been a necessity for making clothes, and handwork offers the possibility of creating with simple and inexpensive tools. Wool is our very own raw material which is brought to perfection through knitting.

We like to think of knitting as the most Norwegian of all crafts, and that our past was influenced by the fact that everyone could knit. This skill was gladly passed from mother to daughter and, as part of past handicraft lessons in schools, knitting was required. Sadly knitting design is no longer a technical school subject here in Norway; therefore, most knitting designers have had background training in another design subject prior to a profession grounded in the handicraft tradition.

Despite this, Norway has always been identified as a knitting nation, and our knitwear is regarded with wonder. Norwegian knitting is associated with traditional patterns and 'Norwegian motifs' which are readily recognized by the rest of the world. Our knitting designs are thriving and can be found at sporting events and on the well-known knitted garments for the tourist and souvenir markets. We have a fantastic knitting tradition but, if that tradition is to continue, there must also be the space and the desire for new expressions of it. These are the areas where designers can offer innovative solutions and be the source for new thinking. We hope that this book will give you that same inspiration, and that there will be many more creative knitting designers in the future.

MARGARETHA FINSETH

Wool is Gold

We are proud to have been able to use only pure, new Norwegian-spun wool for all the designs in this book and have purposively chosen wool which is not treated to be shrink-resistant in any way. So-called machine-washable wool (labelled, for example, 'superwash' or 'machine-washable') has become very popular in the past few years, particularly for its convenience. However, the same treatments ruin some of wool's most important qualities and it is precisely these qualities we desire when we choose to use wool – whether for our Sunday finest or for everyday clothes! When wool has been treated for shrink resistance, the fibre is stretched out and then fixed by various chemical methods; this means that it loses its elastic quality and this its ability to go back to its original shape when it is stretched. At the same time, the wool's ability to absorb water without feeling wet is reduced. The natural crimps in untreated wool fibres create air pockets which hold in heat and give wool a uniquely warm and insulating quality. In addtition, this wool can absorb up to forty per cent of its weight in water without feeling wet against the skin. Together, these distinctive characteristics mean that you stay warm when the wool has become wet, even though you have it next to your body.

Many hours of work go into a hand-knitted garment, and it is a shame when the yarn quality negatively affects the final result. If you knit with untreated yarn, it is easier to produce an even surface and a nice, flat garment in a simple stockinette/stocking stitch or multicoloured pattern knitting. The fibres are more elastic and, thus, can be more easily finished afterwards with steam and heat. Small problems with the gauge/tension can be steamed away. You also avoid the sagging and loss of shape which comes with wearing and washing garments knitted with shrink-resistant wool yarn.

Machine Washing

With knowledge and forethought, one can wash wool in the washing machine. Most washing machines have wool cycles which wash wool garments gently. Wash the garment with the wrong side out, always using soap especially made for wool and silk. After washing, put the garment in a washing bag or pillow case and centrifuge or spin out excess water and then spread it out to finished measurements. If possible dry it flat, or hang it over a large, round beam. A tightly knitted but not-too-heavy of a garment can be dried on a clothes hanger with wide, padded shoulders. However, it is best to keep knitted garments flat.
NOTE: Machine-washing is safest in front-loading machines.

Washing by Hand

In principle, wool garments are hand-washed in the same way, with the same water temperature of 80°F/30°C for washing and rinsing. Do not twist or wring the garment while washing but carefully squeeze the water from the garment. Centrifuge or spin out water and dry garment as described above. Never dry knitted garments in a clothes dryer, and never use chlorine bleach on wool.

Washing Materials for Wool

Beautiful handwork is also a valuable heirloom and, with the right care, your knitted garment will be enjoyed by both you and future generations. We recommend enzyme-free, liquid soaps for wool and silk made with pure plant soaps, natural glycerin and essential plant oils. Wool garments can become dried out after a number of washings, but this can be remedied with a lanolin (natural fat from sheep's wool) rinse which will make the garment soft again.

Steaming

Stockinette/stocking and multicolour pattern knitting can be lightly steamed, but, in principle, one should never steam lace knitting, structural patterns, cables or ribbing. Always steam the garment from the wrong side. Dampen an ironing cloth in lukewarm water, wring out the excess water and then lay the cloth over the garment. Do not put the iron directly on the garment but hold it a little above the cloth, so that the steam seeps down into the wool. At the same time, lightly stretch the garment to finished dimensions.

Blocking

Alternatively, instead of steaming, the knitted pieces can be spread out to finished measurements on a flat surface before the pieces are joined. For example, you can use a large piece of foam board, pinning the pieces to it so that the edges are as even and straight as possible. Lay a damp cloth over the pieces and leave everything until dry.
TIP: If you knit a lot and find yourself blocking pieces often, you can make a more permanent blocking board. Cover a piece of plywood with foam rubber which is about ¾in/2cm thick and then cover the foam and board with cotton fabric which can be stapled down.

Materials

We recommend that you use the yarn which is listed in each pattern. If you are unable to find that yarn, choose one with a similar thickness or number of metres for the same weight as that specified in the pattern. It is best to match both yarn thickness and yardage (yarn grist). Knit a swatch in order to be sure that the gauge/tension is correct.

Gauge/tension

Be sure that you have the same gauge/tension as the pattern specifies. Differences in gauge will affect the size of the garment. Knit a test swatch with the suggested needle size, yarn and pattern. Lightly steam the swatch (see above), lay it on a flat surface and take the measurements in the centre of the swatch. If you have more stitches per 4in/10cm than the pattern specifies, then use larger needles. If you have fewer stitches, change to smaller needles. Although the gauge/tension should be correct for the width and length, it is most important to have the correct number of stitches for the width.
Most people purl more loosely than they knit. If you are working a garment back and forth with the purls on the wrong side, it could be helpful to use a half-size smaller needle on the wrong side than on the right.

Patterns

Read through the whole pattern before you start knitting. If you are unsure whether a garment will fit well, check its measurements against one which you have on hand.

Charts

Knit stitches are rectangular and the charts in the book have squares which show the patterns in the correct proportions to the knitting. We have chosen to use large charts which show whole pieces of garments. If the pattern is too difficult to follow, the charts can be copied and enlarged. It is easier to follow the patterns if you mark your place with self-adhesive note papers. Fasten the paper at the top of the row you are knitting so that you can see if the pattern corresponds to the rows below.

Multicolour Pattern Knitting

In order to maintain the evenness of the motifs when you knit patterns with two or more colours on a row, you should:

- Always knit the different colours in the same order; for example, hold black on one finger while you throw the red yarn. Avoid changing the places of the colours.
- Do not let the yarn draw in on the wrong side when you change colours.
- When the space between colour changes is longer than six to seven stitches with a medium-sized yarn or about eight stitches with a thinner yarn, the yarn must be caught on the wrong side by twisting the two threads around each other. This eliminates long, loosely-hanging threads.
- If you are knitting large pattern motifs against a background colour, always carry both threads around each row. The pattern yarn alternately twists over and under the background yarn about every fifth stitch. This gives the piece a woven effect so that the garment has an even thickness all around and you avoid long threads on the wrong side.

Edges

Unless otherwise stated in the pattern, you can pick up stitches for the neckbands, front bands, etc. on a knitted garment using a crochet hook. With right side facing and the yarn on the wrong side, use the crochet hook to pull up loops through the stitches along the edge. When the hook fills up with stitches, you can slip them back over the hook and onto a knitting needle.

Embroidery

Several of the designs in this book have patterns with details embroidered in either duplicate or chain stitch. Use a blunt needle – for example, a tapestry needle (which can be purchased at a handicraft or needlework store) – and work the embroidery on pieces which have already been steamed.

Duplicate Stitch: Chain Stitch:

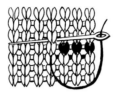   

Three-Needle Bind-Off:

Place stitches to be joined onto two separate needles and hold them with right sides of knitting facing each other. *Using a third needle knit the first stitch on each of the other two needles together as one stitch. Knit next stitch on each needle the same way. Pass first stitch over second stitch. Repeat from * until one stitch remains on third needle. Cut yarn and pull tail through last stitch.

Lice Stitch: alternate sts in light and dark yarn.

Abbreviations

BO	bind off (= British cast off)
cm	centimetre
CO	cast on
dc	double crochet (= British treble crochet)
dec	decrease
dpn	double pointed needle (= British double ended needle)
g	grams
hdc	half double crochet (= British half treble)
inc	increase
K	knit
k2tog	knit two together
k2tog tbl	knit two together through back loops
m	metres
ndl	needle
psso	pass slipped st over
sl	slip
sl st	in crochet, a slip st (= British single crochet)
st	stitch
P	purl
r	row
rnd(s)	round(s)
sc	single crochet (= British double crochet)
tbl	through back loop (makes a twisted stitch)
yd	yard(s)
yo	yarn over (= British yarn forward)
in	after a number = inches

Yarn Specifications

Gjestal Spinneri; Vestlandsgarn – approx. 100m per 50 g	8/4
Hillesvåg Ullvarefabrikk; Hifa 2 – approx. 315m per 100 g	6.3/2
Hillesvåg Ullvarefabrikk; Hifa Trollgarn – approx. 114m per 100 g	2.3/2
Rauma Ullvarefabrikk; Pt4 Kamgarn (worsted yarn) approx. 100m pr 50 g	8/4
Rauma Ullvarefabrikk; Rauma 3-ply Strikkegarn – approx. 108m per 50 g	6.5/3
Rauma Ullvarefabrikk; Istra Kamgarn (worsted yarn) – approx. 105m per 50 g	8.5/4
Rauma Ullvarefabrikkk; Rauma Finnullgarn – approx. 175m per 50 g	7/2
Rauma Ullvarefabrikk; Rauma Vamsegarn – approx. 83m per 50 g	5/3
SandnesGarn; Telemark – appprox. 140m per 50 g	11/4
SandnesGarn; Peer Gynt – approx. 91m per 50 g	9.5/5
SandnesGarn; Heimly – approx. 112m per 50 g	9.5/4

American terms and British equivalents:

baste/basting = tack/tacking
gauge = tension
stockinette = stocking st

DESIGNER'S BACKGROUND AND INSPIRATION

Mette N. Handberg
Born in Bergen in 1944.

Education
Trained at Bergen's Municipal Women's Industry School; Bergen Art-Handicraft School and Ant. Johannesen's Business School.

Professional Work
Mette has run her own workshop since 1968.
She has designed for Jens Hoff Yarns and Concepts; the 1997 Jubilee Sweater, 'Rex Norvegiae', a jacket for the 1997 Trondheim thousand-year jubilee; 'Amadeus', for a collection of handknitted children's sweaters for Sandnes Uldvarefabrik in conjunction with the zoo in Klaebu and Gustav Lorentzen, CD, 'Amadeus'.
She has also woven ecclesiastical textiles for four churches, including Nidaros Cathedral in Trondheim and decorative pieces for, among others, Televerket, Steinkjer and the Tunga County Prison in Trondheim.
She has produced freelance designs for Husflid (the Norwegian handicraft association) and several Norwegian yarn companies.

Awards
1988: First prize for 'Jubilee Sweater', Dale of Norway.
1990: First prize for 'Märtha Louise's Dream Sweater', ALLERS/Dale of Norway.
1995: First prize for 'Thunder Bay', World Cup, Dale of Norway.

Exhibitions
Mette has had ten solo exhibitions, among other venues, the Nordenfjeldske Art-Industry Museum. In 1974, she was Trondheim's representative in Darmstad for tapestry weaving. She was Norway's representative at an exhibition of ecclesiastical textiles at the 1982 Organ Festival in Sorø, Denmark. Her works have also been bought by the Norwegian Culture Council.

On Designing
– At the technical school, I wrote my thesis on Norwegian tapestry weaving. These were older coverings with religious motifs, good and foolish virgins and motifs from the feast. When I wrote my thesis, these cultural treasures were synonymous, for me at least, with museum collections. Little did I know then that tapestry weaving would become my chosen path. Since 1968, I have woven tapestries in one form or another of this decorative pictorial representation.
In 1968, I gradually began designs for knitting. It is exciting for me that these two paths have converged to the degree that they have.
The influence of folk art has become the driving force for my work and is a limitless source for inspiration which can be further developed with experience, knowledge and intelligence. There were several sources of inspiration for 'Virgin' (see pages 8–15). The old weavings have fascinated me since childhood, especially the figures which were almost alike. Around the main motifs were the borders and areas with various decorative designs. There one finds, along with other patterns, the eight-petalled rose which we all enjoy so much. The innkeeper and his wife, who welcome us to the feast, are on the jacket front.

– I have woven a tapestry called 'The Norwegian Bride's Heart' and have also knitted a jacket with the same name and the same look. The jacket was, in turn, the inspiration for the piece entitled 'The Siren's Heart' (see pages 16–23). Sections of this are woven in damask patterning and krokbragd, a boundweave technique used in bedcoverings from many areas of our country. When the jacket is buttoned, the vest underneath becomes like a breastplate. The colours – black, violet, yellow and many shades of red – are also taken from this covering. With the embroideries, this becomes like evening wear for a high occasion and could equally-well be called 'The Siren Bride'.
Earlier it was common to use silver coins as buttons, especially those called 'wigged eight shillings. I have used Norwegian one-øre coins for the buttons here.

METTE N. HANDBERG

The set consists of a jacket, vest, cap and fingerless gloves. The jacket is knitted in the round up to the neck opening and then cut up the centre as are the armhole openings. The vest is knitted in the round up to the neck opening. The top of the cap is knitted back and forth and then stitches are picked up so that the band can be knitted in the round.

SIZES
S (M) L

Jacket:

Total circumference:	46 (48) 50in	117 (122) 127cm
Total length:	26 1/2 (27 1/2) 28 3/4in	67 (70) 73cm
Underarm length:	17 1/4 (17 3/4) 18in	44 (45) 46cm

Vest:

Total circumference:	38 1/4 (41 1/4) 43 1/4in	97 (105) 110cm
Total length:	19 3/4 (21 1/4) 22in	50 (54) 56cm

MATERIALS
Vestland Yarn (100% pure new wool – 100 metres per 50 grams) from Gjestal Spinneri:

Jacket:

black (201)	600 (650) 700 g
dark red (237)	400 (450) 500 g

Vest

black (201)	100 (100) 100 g
dark red (237)	250 (250) 300 g
red (209)	200 (200) 250 g

Fingerless Gloves:

black (201)	50 g or 15 g leftover yarn
dark red (237)	50 g
red (209)	50 g

Cap:

black (201)	50 g or 20 g leftover yarn
dark red (237)	100 g
red (209)	50 g

Needles: circular and double pointed needles sizes 1 (2.5mm) and 2 (3mm) or 4 (3.5mm), or size to obtain correct gauge.

Notions/haberdashery: 8 (9) 9 silver or tin buttons for the jacket; buttonhole thread; bias tape to cover seams on inside.

Gauge/tension: 24 sts and 26 rows = 4 x 4in/10 x 10cm in stockinette stitch and colour pattern on larger ndls.
Be sure that your gauge is correct!

JACKET
Pattern
Chart A shows the right front, B the back, and C the left front – each of these sections has different motifs. Diagram D shows the entire sleeve. The sizes are marked with arrows and dark lines. Follow the arrows and lines marking your size.

Body
With black and circular ndl 2 (3mm), CO 260 (270) 280 sts; join. Change to circular ndl 1 (2.5mm) and, working in the round, knit 15 (17) 18 rows for the lower edge facing. The last 4 sts on the rnd form the steek and will later be cut for the front opening. Next, work the turning (eyelet) row, *K2tog, yo*; repeat *–* until 6 sts remain; end K2tog, K4. Knit 2 more rows after the eyelet row, increasing 18 (20) 22 sts evenly spaced on the 2nd rnd (do not work increases over the 4 steek sts) = 277 (289) 301 sts, including the steek sts. Change to ndls 2 or 4 (3 or 3.5mm) and knit the pattern following charts A, B, and C, starting with rnd 3 (the first two rnds on the charts have already been worked). Begin at the right side of chart A and knit to the arrow for your size on the left side;

place a marker. Knit the back, beginning at the arrow for your size at the right side of chart B and ending at the arrow for your size on the left side of chart B; place a marker. Knit the left front, starting at the arrow for your size at the right side of chart C and ending at the left side of the chart. The last 4 sts on the rnd are the steek which are not worked in pattern and which will later be cut up the centre for the front opening.
NOTE: The minus (–) and plus (+) signs on chart A show where you shorten or lengthen the front for sizes S and L. Do not knit the rows marked – for the small size. For size L, knit an extra row at the + signs.
Continue knitting, following the charts to the armhole. Place a new marker on each side at the arrow for your size which points down towards the armhole on the back. but not in the space between the sections of the chart. BO 12 (13) 12 sts centred over the underarm seam. On the next rnd, CO 4 new sts over those bound-off. These 4 sts form the armhole steek and are not knitted in pattern. Continue knitting in the round. At the same time, work decs at the armhole edges. On the fronts, dec 1 st on each rnd 8 (7) 8 times and 1 st on the alternate rnd once. On the back, dec 1 st on every rnd 4 (2) 1 times, and 1 st on each alternate rnd 7 (9) 10 times. At the neckline, bind off the centre 24 (28) 28 sts on the front (including the steek sts). Continue working back and forth in rows and BO 3-2-1-1-1 sts at the neck edge, decreasing every row. Work even until you reach the 4th row before the shoulders and then, on the next row, BO the centre 31 (35) 35 sts on the back for the neck and then work each side separately. BO 3 sts once at the beginning of the row at the neck edge. At the place indicated by the arrow for your size, place the shoulder sts on a holder.

Sleeves
With black and dpn 2 (3mm), CO 50 (50) 54 sts. Change to dpn 1 (2.5mm) and knit 20 rnds for the cuff facing. Work a turning (eyelet) row – *K2tog, yo*; repeat *–* around. Continue in stockinette. Knit 2 rnds with black, increasing to 55 (59) 59 sts on the second rnd, spacing the increases evenly around. Change to dpn 2 or 4 (3 or 3.5mm) and continue, following chart D and working the sts between the arrows for your size and beginning at rnd 3 (the first two rnds have already been completed). When the cuff has been worked, inc to 71 (77) 83 sts, spacing the increases evenly, but without working any increases on the centre 15 sts. On the 6th rnd, inc 2 sts centred at the underarm and then inc 2 sts at the underarm, every 4th rnd until there are 117 (123) 129 sts on ndls. At the arrow for your size, BO 6 sts centred at the underarm, and then work the sleeve cap back and forth in rows. At the beginning of each row for each side, dec 3 sts 4 (5) 6 times, 2 sts 10 times, and 3 sts 5 (4) 3 times. BO the rest of the sts on the right side.

Finishing
Spread the pieces to the correct measurements, lay flat between damp towels, and leave until dry. Machine-stitch 2 lines on each side of the centre of each steek. Cut up the centre of each steek between the machine-stitched lines. Turn the facings for the body and sleeve cuffs to the inside and sew them loosely to the wrong side. Put the shoulder sts for the front and back pieces onto separate ndls 2 (3mm) and work 3 needle bind-off.
Neckband: With black, ndl 1 (2.5mm), and right side facing, pick up and knit about 116 (120) 124 sts around the neck opening. Knit one row (wrong side) and then 4 rows in stockinette (beginning with a knit row on the right side); an eyelet row for the turning as at the bottom of the jacket body (begin and end row with K2tog); finish with 4 rows stockinette for the facing. BO loosely. Turn the facing to the inside and sew it to the wrong side.
Front Buttonband (left front): With black, ndl 1 (2.5mm), and right side of the left front facing, pick up and knit about 12 sts for every 2in/5cm. Knit one row on the wrong side and then work 9 rows stockinette (beginning with a knit row on the right side). Knit one row on the wrong side for the turning row and then work 9 more rows in stockinette for the facing. BO.
Front Buttonhole band (right front): Work as for the left front, making 8 (9) 9 buttonholes on the 5th row, spacing the buttonholes evenly, beginning about 1/2in/1.5cm from the neck edge and ending 3/4in/2cm from the lower edge. For each buttonhole, BO 3 sts and then CO 3 new sts over the bound-off sts on the next row. Work corresponding buttonholes in the facing.

Turn the facings to the inside and sew them loosely to the wrong side. Using a single ply of yarn, sew around each buttonhole. Sew in the sleeves with back stitch on wrong side. Sew on bands of bias tape to cover the raw seams on the inside. Lightly steam the garment from the wrong side and sew on the buttons.

VEST

Pattern

Chart E shows the front, F shows half of the back. The sizes are marked with arrows and dark lines. Follow the arrows and lines marking your size.

With dark red and ndl 2 (3mm), CO 198 (210) 222 sts; join. Change to ndl 1 (2.5mm) and knit 18 rnds in stockinette for the lower edge facing. Change to black and knit an eyelet row for the turning by working *K2tog, yo*; repeat *-* around. Continue in stockinette. With dark red, knit 2 rnds, increasing to 212 (224) 236 sts on the second rnd, spacing the increases evenly around. Change to ndl 2 or 4 (3 or 3.5mm) and knit the pattern following the charts, beginning at rnd 3 (the first two rnds have already been completed). Begin at the arrow for your size at the right side of chart E and knit to the arrow for your size on the left side (= front). Begin at the arrow for your size on the right side of chart F, work to the centre, and then back from left to right so that the pattern is reversed (= back). The black stripes on each side of the star pattern at the centre are knitted as follows: Add a separate length of black for each stripe. Knit to the black sts; lay the two red strands over to the left; knit the two black sts; lay the black over to the left; bring the two reds over the black and continue following the chart. When you have worked the last black stripe in the lower edge, continue following the charts, but add in a length of black on each side and knit 1 side st with black in the same way as you worked the black sts at the centre of the lower edge. The sts worked with black are marked on the chart for size L only. **NOTE:** on sizes S and M, the first and last sts on chart E should also be knitted with a black side st. Inc 1 st on each side of the side seam every 10 rnds until you have 232 (252) 264 sts. **NOTE:** On size S there is a repeat at the right which is not knitted. At the arrow for the armhole, BO 21 (23) 23 sts centred at each underarm. On the next rnd, CO 3 new sts over the bound-off sts for the armhole steek and continue knitting in the round. The steek sts are not knitted in pattern. Dec 1 st on each side of the steek on every rnd 5 (6) 6 times. At the arrow marking the neck, BO the centre 29 sts on the front. On the next rnd, CO 3 new sts over the bound-off sts for the neck steek and continue knitting in the round. The steek sts are not worked in pattern. Dec 1 st at each side of the neck steek on every rnd 5 times. At the arrow for the neckline, BO the centre 33 sts on the back and knit each side separately, working back and forth. Bind off another 3 sts at the beginning of the neck edge row. Finish the pattern at the arrow for your size and then work 1 row with black. Place the shoulder sts on a holder.

Finishing

Machine-stitch two lines on each side of the centre of the neck and armhole steeks and cut each steek between the machine-stitched lines. Spread the vest out to the correct measurements, lay flat between damp towels, and leave until dry. Place the shoulder sts onto separate ndls and work the three-needle bind-off with black yarn. Turn the lower edge facing to the inside and sew it loosely to the wrong side.

Neckband: With black, ndl 1 (2.5mm), and right side facing, pick up and knit about 140 sts around the neck opening; join. Purl 1 rnd and then work 4 rows stockinette. On the 1st and 3rd rnds of stockinette, dec 2 sts at each corner with 2 sts in-between: K2tog tbl, K2, K2tog (= 8 decs on each dec row). Purl 1 row on the right side for the turning and then work 4 rows stockinette for the facing, working increases on rows 2 and 4 at the points where you decreased on the front of the neck edge. BO loosely. Turn the facing to the inside and sew it loosely on the wrong side.

Armhole bands: With black and ndl 1 (2.5mm), pick up and knit 116 (120) 120 sts around the armhole; join. Purl 1 rnd and then work 4 rnds stockinette.

On the 1st and 3rd rnds of stockinette, dec by K2tog in each corner and at the centre of the underarm (= 3 decs per rnd). Purl 1 rnd for the turning and then work 4 rnds stockinette for the facing, increasing on rnds 2 and 4 at the points where you decreased on the front of the band. BO loosely. Turn the facing to the inside and sew it loosely on the wrong side. Lightly steam the vest on the wrong side.

FINGERLESS GLOVES

Pattern

Chart G shows the pattern for the left glove.

With dark red and dpn 2 (3mm), CO 36 sts. Change to dpn 1 (2.5mm) and, working in the round, knit 14 rnds. Change to red and increase 8 sts evenly spaced around. Change to dpn 2 (3mm) and work the pattern following chart G, starting with the 2nd rnd (the first rnd has already been worked). Increase for the thumb gusset as the chart shows by picking up the strand before or after the edge st on each side of the thumb gusset: place the strand on the left ndl and knit it through the back. Continue following the chart until there are 9 sts for the thumb gusset. At the place indicated by the arrow, place the thumb sts on a holder. CO 9 new sts over the thumbhole and continue knitting in the round, following the chart. The dark red on the back of the hand can be knitted in red and embroidered with duplicate st later or it can be knit in, using short lengths of yarn for each motif. When the charted pattern has been completed, change to dpn 1 (2.5mm) and continue knitting with dark red for 2 rows or desired length to base of little finger. On the next rnd, BO the last 5 sts on ndl 2 and the first 5 sts on ndl 3 = 10 sts for the little finger. CO 2 new sts over the bound-off sts on the next rnd and knit another 2 rnds. BO. Place the thumb sts onto dpn 1 (2.5mm) and, with dark red, pick and knit 9 sts at the back of the thumb opening. Knit 6 rnds in stockinette, then 2 rnds with K1/P1 ribbing. BO loosely in ribbing. Work a row of single crochet around the opening, fastening between the fingers. Steam carefully, but not over the cuff. The lower edge of the cuff will roll up. Knit the right mitten in the same way, reversing the position of thumb gusset and fingers.

CAP

Pattern

Chart H shows the crown and chart I shows the pattern for cap band.

With dark red and straight ndls 2 (3mm), CO 27 sts for the crown. Work back and forth in stockinette, following chart H. **NOTE:** The first row of the pattern is the cast-on row. Increase at the beginning and end of each row as shown on the chart. At the beginning of the row, inc by casting on 1 new st and at the end of the row, inc by knitting into the front and back of the last st. The red in the star at the centre of the crown can be knitted with dark red and embroidered with duplicate st afterwards. On the dec rows, BO 1 st at the beginning of the row and knit the last 2 sts together. The last row on the pattern chart is the binding-off row. Steam the crown lightly and work the duplicate sts in red on the star, as indicated on the chart.

With dark red, pick up and knit 27 sts on each of the crown's straight edges and 28 sts on each of the diagonal edges = 220 sts; join. Knit 18 rows, working in the round. Decrease on the next rnd: *K2 tog, K2*; repeat *-* around. Knit 2 rnds without decreasing. Decrease on the next rnd: *K1, K2tog*; repeat *-* around = 110 sts remain. Knit 1 more rnd with dark red. Then work the pattern for the band by following chart I. Beginning at the arrow, knit the centre motif over 13 sts and then the left-leaning diagonal stripes over 49 sts (the repeat is indicated by *-*). For the last 48 sts of the rnd, work the right-leaning diagonal stripes, beginning at the right hand side of chart I and repeating from *-* across the 48 sts. After the last 2 rnds with black, change to red and knit an eyelet row for the turning: *K2tog, yo*; repeat *-* around. On the next rnd, knit the knit sts from the previous rnd and slip each yo and make a new yo, so that there are doubled strands. Knit all the sts on the next rnd, working the doubled yo strands as one. Using the same colour and ndls, on the next rnd, dec every 10th st by K2tog. Continue working the facing in stockinette st until it is the same length as the edging, then BO loosely. Turn the facing at the eyelet row and sew it on the inside. Steam the cap carefully.

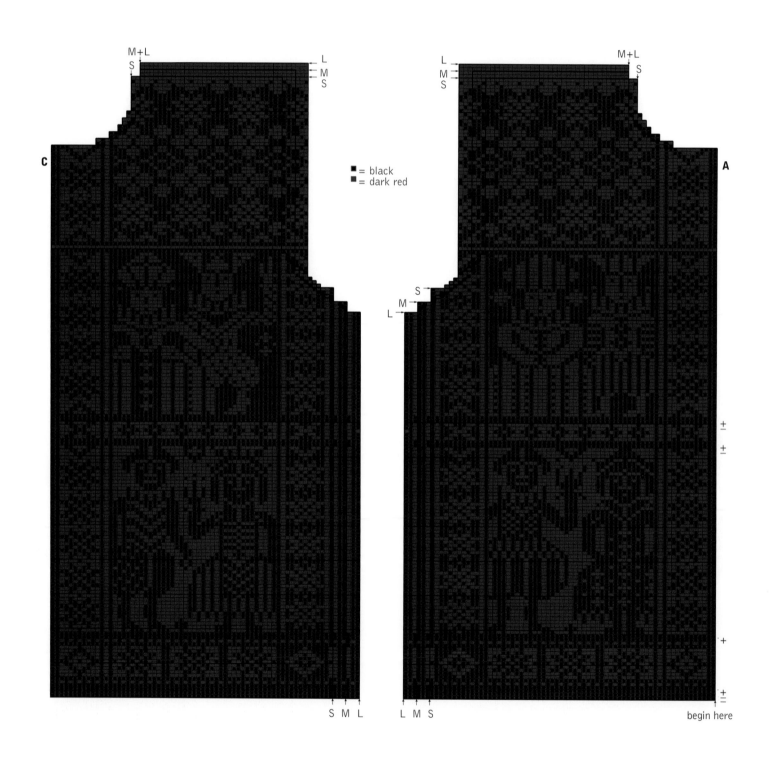

C

A

M+L
S

L
M
S

L
M
S

M+L
S

= black
= dark red

S
M
L

S M L

L M S

begin here

JOMFRU 'VIRGIN'

METTE N. HANDBERG

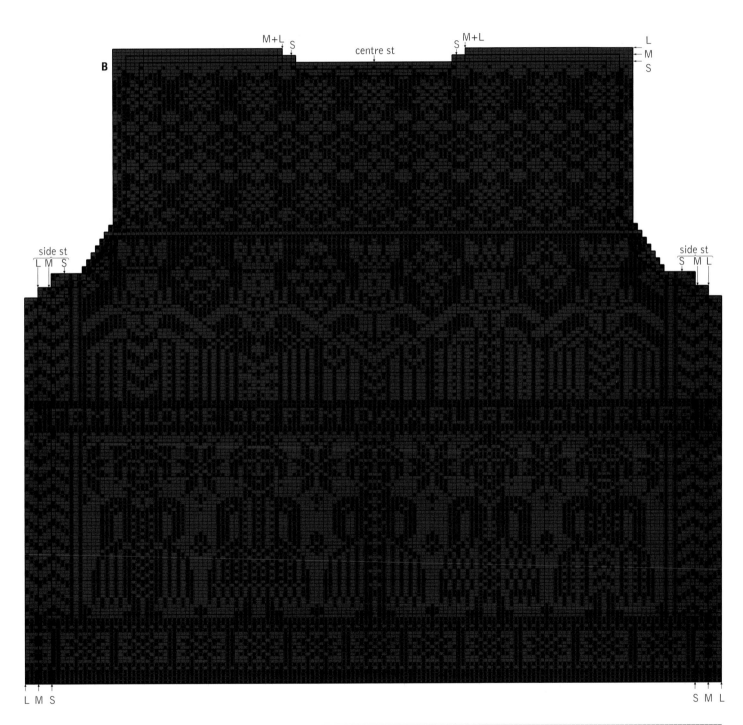

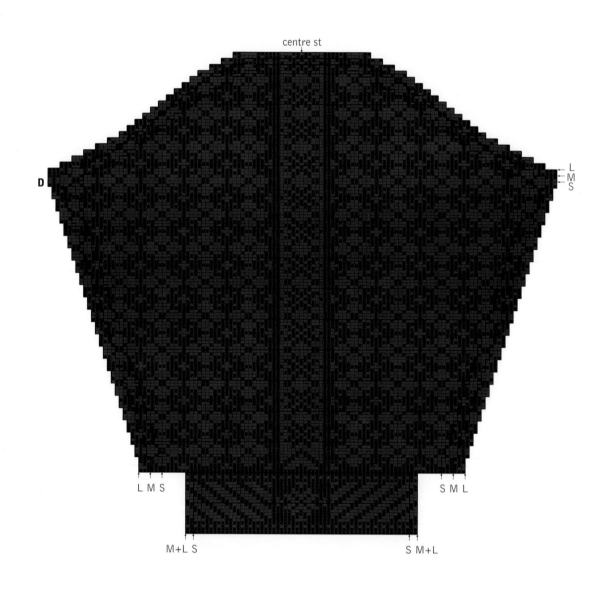

centre st

D

L
M
S

L M S

S M L

M+L S

S M+L

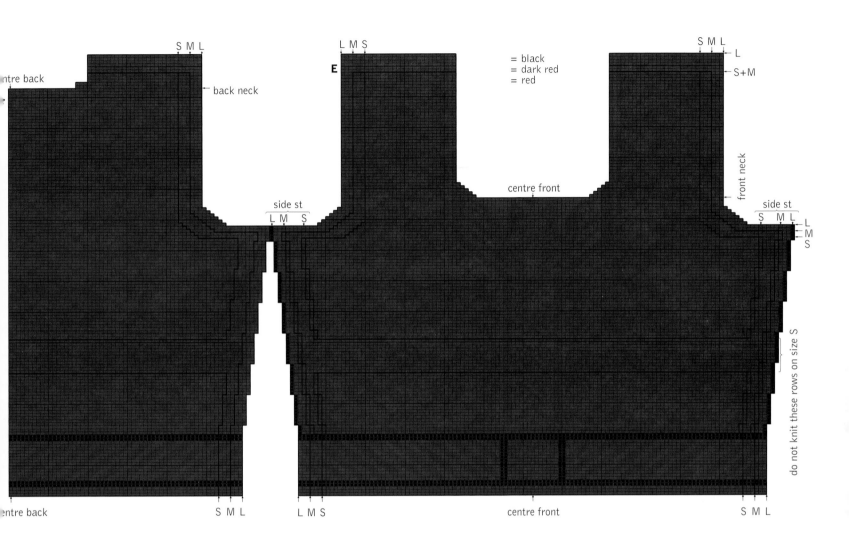

= black
= dark red
= red

■ = black
■ = dark red
■ = red

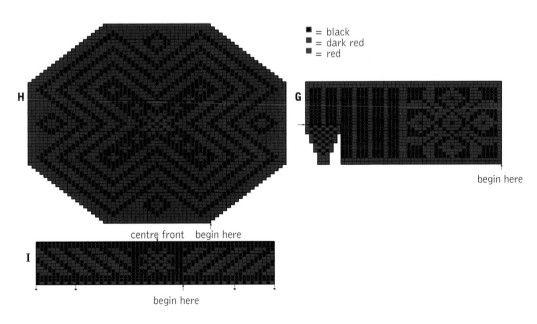

METTE N. HANDBERG

The set consists of a jacket, vest, cap, fingerless gloves, and socks. The jacket is knitted in the round up to the neck opening and then cut up the centre front as are the armholes. The vest is knitted in two parts. The body is knitted in the round to the armholes and cut open; the centre front insert is worked back and forth and sewn to the body afterwards.

SIZES
S (M) L
Jacket:

Total circumference:	40 1/2 (42 1/2) 44in	103 (108) 112cm
Total length:	19 3/4 (21 1/4) 22 1/2 ins	50 (54) 60cm
Underarm length:	17 3/4 (19) 20 in	45 (48) 51cm

VEST

Total circumference:	35 1/2 (37 1/2) 39 1/2in	90 (95) 100cm
Total length:	17 (17 3/4) 18 1/2in	43 (45) 47cm

MATERIALS
Telemark (100% pure new wool – 140 metres per 50 grams) from SandnesGarn:

Jacket:

dark red (645)	350 (400) 450 g
red (641)	400 (450) 450 g
black (612)	100 (100) 150 g
flag red (643)	50 (50) 100 g
orange (634)	50 (50) 50 g
yellow (617)	50 (50) 50 g
pink (654)	50 (50) 50 g

Vest:

dark red (645)	50 (100) 100 g
red (641)	150 (200) 250 g
black (612)	50 (100) 100 g

+ the leftover flag red (643) and orange (634)

Socks:

dark red (645)	100 g
red (641)	100 g
black (612)	50 g

+ the leftover flag red (643), orange (634) and pink (654)

Cap:

dark red (645)	50 g
red (641)	50 g
black (612)	50 g

Fingerless Gloves:

dark red (645)	50 g
red (641)	50 g
black (612)	50 g

(or the leftover yarns from the other garments)
The embroidery on the vest, cap and gloves is worked with single plies of the yarn colours used on the jacket.
Needles: circular and dpn 1 (2.5mm), 2 (3mm), and 4 (3.5mm).
Notions/haberdashery: 6 small silver or tin buttons for the jacket. The jacket pictured here used buttons of old one-øre coins backed by a brass stud.
Gauge/tension: 26 sts and 27/28 rows = 4 x 4in/10 x 10cm in stockinette st and colour pattern on ndls 2 (3mm).
Be sure that your gauge is correct! Change to larger or smaller ndls if necessary.

JACKET
Pattern
Chart A shows the body front and back; B is the pattern for the inside of the cuffs on the sleeves; C shows the whole sleeve; D is the pattern for the cuffs; E is the pattern for the armhole bands. The sizes for the body are marked with arrows and dark lines. Follow the arrows and lines marking your size. On the pattern rows where 3 colours are used, change to ndls 4 (3.5mm) so that the piece doesn't draw in.

Body
With dark red and ndls 1 (2.5mm), CO 225 (237) 249 sts; join. Knit in the round until the piece measures 1 1/2in/4cm, increasing to 244 (256) 268 sts on the last rnd, spacing the incs evenly around. Knit one more rnd after the inc rnd and then work a rnd of holes (eyelet) for the turning: *K2tog, yo*; repeat *–* around. **NOTE:** Do not work the eyelet sts over the last 4 sts on the rnd which form the centre front steek; instead, begin and end the rnd with K2tog on each side of these 4 sts.
Change to ndls 2 (3mm) and continue by following the pattern on chart A. After the steek sts, begin the right front at the place indicated by the arrow and work to the arrow for your size on the left side of the chart. Knit 2 sts (= side sts) before you begin the back: starting at the arrow for your size on the right side of the chart, work across to the arrow for your size at the left of the chart. Knit 2 sts (= side sts) and then work the left front, beginning at the arrow for your size at the right side of the chart and ending at the place marked 'end left front'. The 4 last sts on the rnd are the steek sts and are knitted with a doubled strand (each of the pattern yarns held together). If you are changing colours at the centre of the steek, it is not necessary to weave in the ends – just leave a 2in/5cm tail hanging. The side sts are always worked in black. After the first black pattern band, knit the side sts with black up to the armhole in this manner: Using a separate strand of black, lay it in before the 2 side sts, then twist the other pattern yarns over it towards the left. Knit the 2 side sts with black; lay the black yarn over towards the left; then bring the pattern yarns around it and continue the rnd.
Inc 1 st on each side of the side sts as shown on the chart.
For the V-neck, BO 1 st on each side of the centre front steek every 3rd rnd 19 (20) 21 times. At the arrow marking the underarm, BO the side sts, and CO 4 new sts over the bound-off sts on the next rnd for the armhole steek and continue working in the round. The steek sts are worked with doubled yarn but not in pattern for the entire length.
When 8 (10) 10 rnds remain before the shoulders, BO the centre 37 (37) 39 sts on the back for the neck and work the rest of the body back and forth. At the beginning of each neck edge row, dec as shown on the chart. Finish the pattern at the arrow for your size and then work one row with black. Place the sts on a holder.

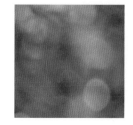

Sleeves
With black and dpn 1 (2.5mm), CO 66 sts; join. Work the striped pattern in the round for the cuff facing, following chart B. Continuing with black, work 2 rnds in stockinette, increasing to 72 sts on the first rnd, with incs evenly spaced around. Then work an eyelet rnd for the turning: *K2tog, yo*; repeat *–* around. Change to ndls 2 (3mm) and knit 1 rnd, increasing to 73 sts. Continue, following chart C. Using a long strand, knit the first and last underarm st on each rnd with black in the same manner as the side sts on the body. Inc 1 st on each side of the centre 2 underarm sts as shown on the chart. Finish the sleeve at the arrow for your size. BO loosely. You can also knit the jacket as a vest by omitting the sleeves.

Finishing

Machine-stitch two lines on each side of the centre of the armhole and front steeks on the body and cut between the lines. Spread the garment out to the correct measurements, lay flat between damp towels, and leave until dry. Weave the shoulder sts together with black yarn. Turn the facings for the lower edge and cuffs to the inside and sew them loosely to the wrong side.

Neck and Front bands: With black, ndls 1 (2.5mm), and right side facing, pick up and knit 6 sts for every 7 rows along the right front, around the neck and down the left side. Knit one row on the wrong side and then follow the pattern on chart D. At the same time, on each right side row, dec 2 sts at each corner of the shoulders 5 times: work until 3 sts from the corner where the neck and shoulder meet, K2tog tbl, K1, K2tog. After the dec rows are completed, knit one row on the wrong side for the turning, and then, with red, work 9 rows stockinette for the facing. Work increases to correspond with the decreases on the front of the band. BO loosely. Turn the band to the inside and sew it loosely on the wrong side.

Armhole bands: With black, ndls 1 (2.5mm), and right side facing, pick up and knit 6 sts for every 7 rows as for the front band. Working in the round, purl one row then work the pattern on chart E. Continue with black and purl one row for the turning, then knit 5 rnds for the facing. BO loosely. Set the sleeves into the armhole, wrong sides facing and aligning the armhole's raw edge edge-to-edge with the bound-off edge of the sleeve. Turn the facing over the raw edge and sew it down through all the layers. The sleeve is sewn at the same time with the facing and the facing lies as a loose edge outside the sleeve on the right side. Sew the buttons on the left front band, with the lowest about 3/4in/2cm from the bottom edge and the top button about 3/8in/1cm below the V-neck; the other buttons are placed evenly in-between.

Make buttonhole loops on the right front band, using a heavy thread for the loops. With yarn in the same colour as the band, sew buttonhole sts around the loops. Use the same number of sts for each buttonhole loop. Carefully steam the jacket from the wrong side.

VEST

Pattern

Chart F shows the front and back of the body, chart G shows the front insert which is knitted separately, and H shows the pattern for the bands. Sizes are marked with arrows and dark lines. Follow the arrows and lines marking your size.

Body

With dark red and ndls 1 (2.5mm), CO 176 (188) 200 sts; join. Work in the round, following chart F as follows: Beginning at the arrow indicating the right front, work to the left side of the chart, ending at the arrow for your size; place a marker in the last st (= side st). Work the back, starting at the arrow for your size at the right side of the chart and ending at the arrow for your size at the left side of the chart; place a marker in the last st (= side st). Work the left side starting at the arrow for your size at the right side of the chart and ending at the arrow marking the end of the left front. The remaining 3 sts form the front steek. The steek sts are always knitted without any patterning. After 4 rnds, change to ndls 2 (3mm). Continue in pattern, following the chart, increasing at each side as indicated on the chart. **NOTE:** Do not work purl st blocks next to the side sts – work those closest to the seam in knit sts as shown for size L.

At the arrow indicating the armhole for your size, BO 10 (10) 11 sts on each side – 8 (8) 9 on the front, + 1 side st + 1 st from the back. Complete the rnd and cut the yarn. Work each front and the back separately, working back and forth. Begin the rows at the underarm.

Front: Work back and forth without further decreasing until reaching the arrow marking the shoulder for your size. BO the 3 steek sts and place the shoulder sts on a holder.

Back: Working back and forth, dec at the beginning of each row at the armhole edge 2 sts 2 (2) 3 times and 1 st 3 (3) 2 times.

At the arrow marking the neck for your size, BO the 3 centre sts and then work each side separately. Continue, working the decreases for the V-neck as shown on the chart. Place the shoulder sts on a holder when you reach the arrow for your size.

Front Inset

With dark red and ndls 2 (3mm), CO 43 (45) 49 sts. Work back and forth, following chart G on the sts between the arrows for your size (the first row is the wrong side). Work the heart pattern with a separate strand and twist the yarns around each other on the wrong side on every row of the colour changes, so that there will not be any holes in the garment.

The vertical stripes on each side of the flower are shown on the chart for size L, but corresponding stripes should be worked for sizes S and M. At the arrow indicating the neck, place the centre 25 (27) 31 sts on a holder and work each side separately. Place another 4 and then 3 sts onto holders at the places indicated on the chart. After completing the rows on the chart, change to red. Knit 3 rows over all the sts (the 2nd row is knitted on the wrong side and becomes the turning row). Change to black and K2tog at the beginning and and ending on the next row. Work another 5 rows in stockinette for the facing and then BO loosely.

Finishing

Machine-stitch two lines on each side of the centre of the front steek and cut up the front between the lines. Carefully steam the garment on the wrong side. Weave the shoulder sts together.

Front bands: With dark red and ndls 1 (2.5mm) and right side facing, pick up and knit about 281 (297) 313 sts along the front edges and around the neck as follows: beginning at the lower edge of the right front, pick up and knit 106 (114) 122 sts; continue along the neck edge picking up and knitting 69 sts (including the 3 sts at the centre of the V-neck); then pick up and knit 106 (114) 122 sts down the left front. Work 8 rows back and forth following chart H – knit the first row on the wrong side, and then continue in stockinette. At the same time, dec 2 sts at each side of the centre of the back's V-neck on each right side row: K3tog through back loops before the centre and K3tog after the centre. Also dec 2 sts at the shoulders on the 6th and 8th rows: K2tog tbl before the st at the shoulder seam, K1, K2tog.

When the pattern rows have been completed, knit one row on the wrong side for the turning. Change to dark red and work 7 rows in stockinette for the facing, but, on the first row, alternate 1 red and 1 dark red st. At the same time, inc 2 sts at each shoulder seam on rows 1 and 3 and 2 sts at each side of the centre of the V-neck on rows 1, 3, 5, and 7. BO with purl sts.

Sleeve bands: With dark red, short circular ndl 1 (2.5mm) and right side facing, pick up and knit about 13 sts for each 2in/5cm; join. Begin at the centre of the underarm and knit up 1 extra st at the centre of the corner with the front. You should have an even number of sts for the band. Work 7 rnds following chart H (1 rnd less than the front band) with the first rnd purled and the rest knitted. At the same time, starting on the purl rnd, dec 1 st at each side of the corner on every row 6 times in all. Purl 1 rnd for the turning and, with red, knit 6 rnds for the facing, increasing at the corners to correspond with the decs on the band. BO loosely with purl sts. Turn the facing to the inside and sew it loosely to the wrong side.

Front inset: Carefully steam the inset. Embroider around the heart and flower with single-ply yarns as shown in the photo – the contour lines are each worked in a different colour in backstitch with the lines close together so that they resemble chain st.

Pin the inset under the front bands of the front, so that the pieces lie edge-to-edge at the bottom and the outer edge of the inset touches the bound-off edge of the facing. Sew the pieces together with a single-ply yarn, making small stitches from the wrong side. Insert the needle well down through the layers so that it picks up the the raw edge inside the facing but does not go all the way through to the right side. Sew the openings of the band together at the same time as you sew it to the lower edge on the inset. The front inset should lie totally flat under the front edges.

'THE SIREN'S HEART'

METTE N. HANDBERG

SOCKS
Pattern

Chart I shows the left sock with the instep, J shows the left sole and K the right sole. The little heart is embroidered on the big toe after the knitting is completed. You can adapt the charts J and K to knit alternative numbers, if you wish.

With dark red and dpn 1 (2.5mm), CO 72 sts; join. Divide the sts evenly onto 4 ndls with the same number of sts on each ndl. Following chart I, work 4 rnds and then change to dpn 2 (3mm). Continue following the pattern on the chart. After completing the black border pattern, use a separate strand of black to knit the black sts at the centre back of the sock (= marking sts). Knit these sts as in the same way as the side sts on the body of the jacket. BO at the heel at each side of the 3 centre back sts as shown on the chart.

Change to dpn 1 (2.5mm) and knit the heel with black as follows: Knit the 3 centre back sts, then K 15; turn, slip 1 st purlwise, P 32. Place the remaining sts on a holder for the instep. Turn the work, sl 1 st knitwise; knit across until 2 sts remain; turn, sl 1 st purlwise, purl across to the last 2 sts; turn. Continue in this manner, leaving 1 st more on each side of the ndl when the work is turned. Work until there are 10 sts on each side of the needle and 13 sts at the centre. Knit across, until there is 1 st left on the ndl; turn and purl back until there is 1 st left on the other side; turn and K 10. Add red and knit the vertical stripes over the centre 13 sts on on the ndl as follows: alternately K 1 st of each colour, beginning and ending with black. Turn, P 13 sts in stripes. Turn and continue with the stripes over the centre 13 sts, but work 1 st more for every row each time you turn (the new sts are worked in black throughout) until all the sts are used. Cut yarn.

Change to dpn 2 (3mm) and divide the sts so that there are 16 sts on each ndl. The black marking st on the left side of the instep on chart I is the first st on ndl 1. Add in a black strand for the marking st. Work in the round, following chart J for the sole of the foot, add a black strand for the marking st, and knit the instep following chart I. Work the black side sts as for the centre back sts on the leg. At the arrow for the big toe, place 19 sts on a holder – 9 sts from the sole of the foot and 10 sts from the instep. CO 3 new sts over those set aside and continue working in the round, following the chart. Dec on each side of the side sts as shown on the left side of the chart, working the decreases on the right side of the chart in the same way as indicated. Work the big toe with black as follows: Knit 15 rnds, then rnds of K2tog, K1 until 8 sts remain. Cut yarn, draw it through the remaining sts and fasten it on the inside. Embroider a heart on the top of the toe with duplicate st and finish by working 2 rows of back st around it with a single ply of the yarn.

If you want a regular finishing for the sock, do not set aside the sts for the big toe. Instead, dec for the sock toe as shown on each side. You can lengthen the foot by knitting extra diamond patterns before beginning with the black for the toe. Knit the other sock in the same way, but use chart K for the sole and knit the big toe on the opposite side.

FINGERLESS GLOVES
Pattern

Chart L shows the left glove. You can adapt the charts to knit alternative numbers, if you wish.

With dark red and dpn 1 (2.5mm), CO 40 sts; join. Divide the sts evenly onto 4 ndls and knit 14 rows in the round. On the next to the last rnd, inc to 53 sts. Change to dpn 2 (3mm) and continue by following the pattern on chart I. Inc for the thumb gusset as shown. At the arrow, place the 11 thumb sts on a holder. CO 11 new sts over the opening and continue knitting in the round following the chart. When you've completed the rnds on the chart, change to dark red and dpn 1 (2.5mm). BO 13 sts for the little finger (= 7 sts on the front and 6 sts from the palm of the glove). On the next rnd, CO 1 st over the bound-off sts. Knit 1 more rnd and BO loosely.

Thumb: Put the 11 thumb sts onto dpn 2 (3mm) and, with dark red, pick up and knit 11 more sts at the back of the thumbhole. Knit 1 rnd and then work 8 rnds of K1 P1 ribbing. BO loosely. Embroider the top of the glove as shown in the picture, with single plies of yarn. Try on the glove and mark the spot between each finger. Single crochet around each finger, working 1 row around the little finger and 2 rows around each of the other fingers.

Knit the other glove in the same manner, but reverse the position of the thumb and fingers – the vertical stripes should be on the palm side of the glove.

CAP
Pattern

Chart M shows the cap pattern.

With black and ndls 2 (3mm), CO 108 sts; join. Working in the round, knit 18 rnds and then follow the pattern on chart M: beginning at the right side of the chart, repeat the marked section from *–* 6 times altogether; knit the centre motif over 36 sts; continue working *–* on the left side of the chart 6 times. After completing the rnds on the chart, continue with dark red. At the same time, decrease as follows: Rnd 1: *K 10, K2tog*; repeat from *–* around. Knit 2 rnds without decreasing. Rnd 4: *K 9, K2tog*; repeat from *–* around. Continue in the same manner, working one st less between decreases on rnds 7, 9, and 11 and then dec on every rnd until 9 sts remain. Cut yarn, leaving a 5–6in/13–15cm tail; thread the tail through the remaining sts and fasten it on the wrong side. Steam the cap carefully and embroider it, using single plies of the yarn, as shown in the picture.

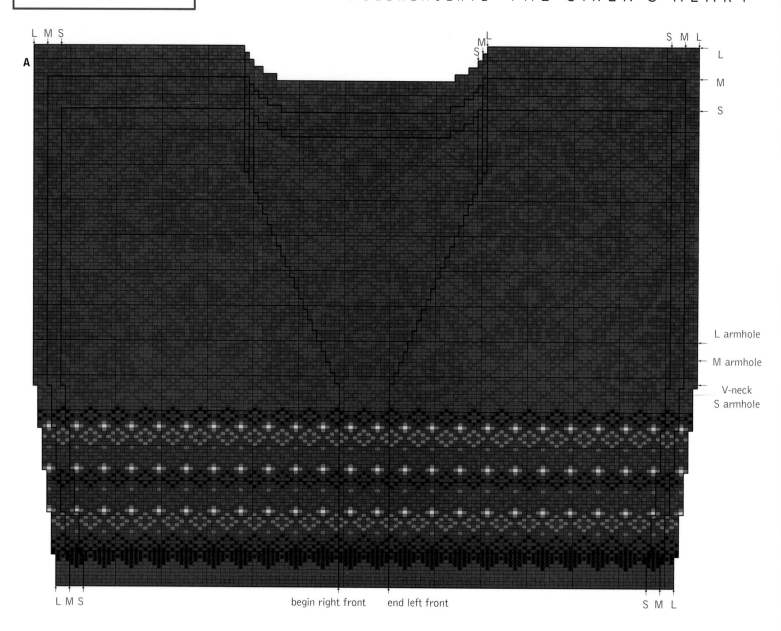

A

L M S

L
M
S

L armhole

M armhole

V-neck
S armhole

L M S

begin right front   end left front

S M L

Fingerless gloves

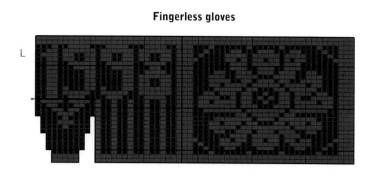

L

Cap

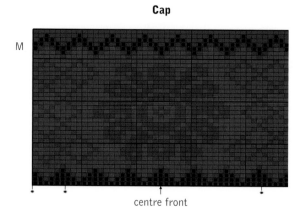

M

centre front

HULDREHJERTE 'THE SIREN'S HEART'

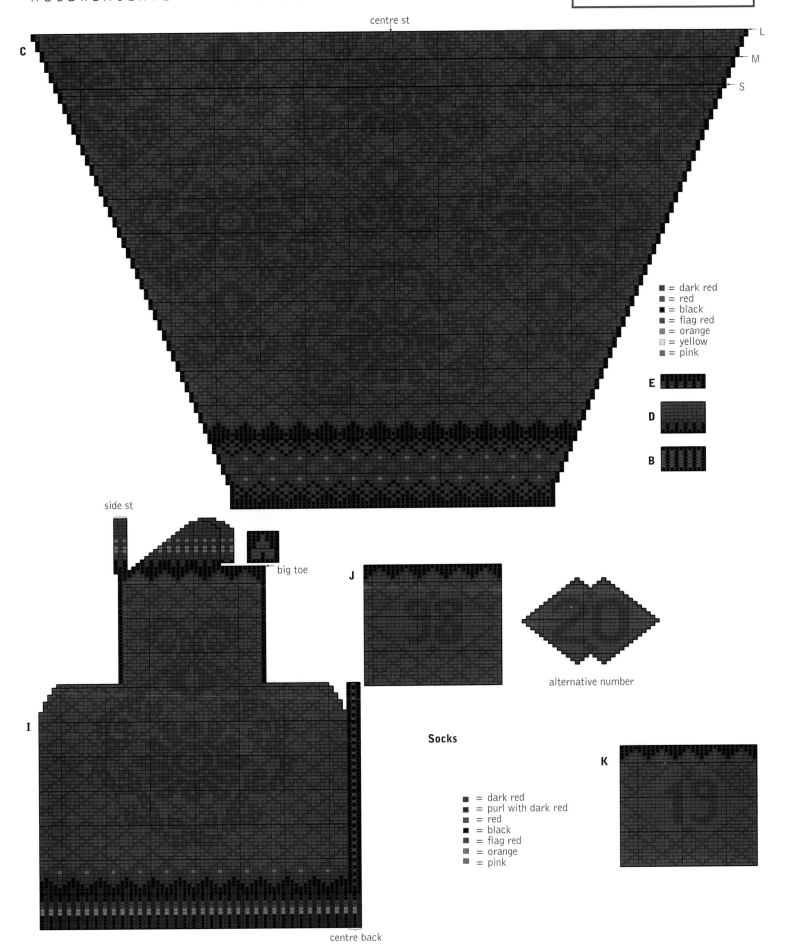

centre st

C

L

M

S

■ = dark red
■ = red
■ = black
■ = flag red
■ = orange
□ = yellow
■ = pink

E

D

B

side st

big toe

J

alternative number

I

Socks

■ = dark red
■ = purl with dark red
■ = red
■ = black
■ = flag red
■ = orange
■ = pink

K

centre back

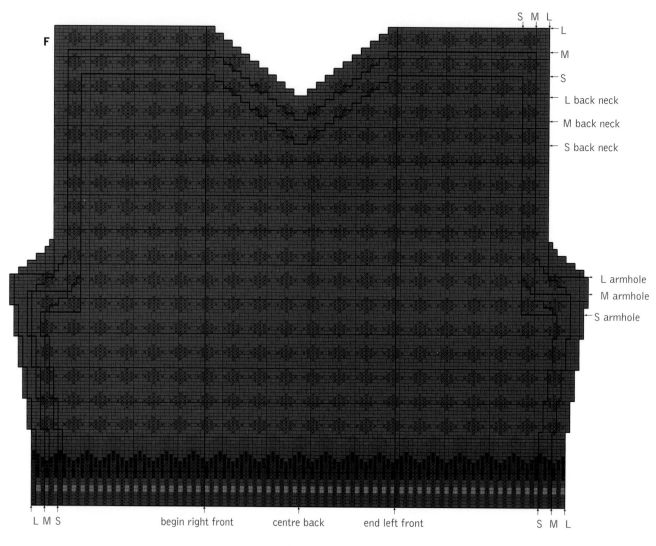

F

S M L
— L
— M
— S
— L back neck
— M back neck
— S back neck

— L armhole
— M armhole
— S armhole

L M S   begin right front   centre back   end left front   S M L

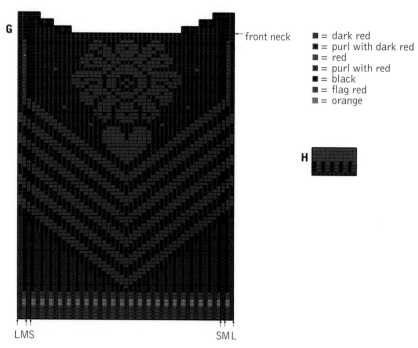

G

— front neck

■ = dark red
■ = purl with dark red
■ = red
■ = purl with red
■ = black
■ = flag red
■ = orange

H

LMS   SML

DESIGNER'S BACKGROUND AND INSPIRATION

Lise Kolstad
Born in 1964.

Education
Trained at the National Handicraft and Art-Industry School.

Publications
Co-author with Tone Takle of: *Sweaters, More Sweaters,*
and Small Sweaters.

Professional Work
Since 1990, Lise has worked with design and concept development
for knitting, clothing and interiors. At the same time, she has worked
with artistic projects for Eterna, a group of artists.
She supervised designs for the silk collection, Kolina, from 1995
until 1997.
Artistic embellishment for Oslo Energy in 1994 and Elverum Teacher's
College in 1996.

Exhibitions
Solo Exhibit: 'Time', The Crypt, Oslo Cathedral, 1993.
Group Exhibits: 'Taiga', Forestry Museum, Elverum 1991; 'Crossing
Point', Henie Onstad's Art Centre, Høvikodden, 1991; 'National Fall
Exhibit', 1992 and 'Talent Exchange', Munich, 1993.

On Designing
– For me, working with knitting design is a balance between play and
seriousness. The intuitive unfolds in certain directions with professional
reflection. One seeks aesthetic qualities in order to mark one's way with
personal characteristics.

At the same time, one can be certain of being a part of the folk art
tradition. The tradition is like a crossbeam which cannot be broken. It
supports one on new paths. The challenge lies in creating something new
while maintaining what others have done before.

– Design is concerned with renewing nature in all one's practices. It
means letting oneself become inspired by the audacity of previous artists
in creating folk art's fruitful variety. By opening the senses, that which
was static embraces new impulses from contemporary trends, traditional
ways, or decorative languages from foreign lands.
A curious person searches for beauty. Fragments are stored like small
pictures in the mind's treasure chest – a charming colour, a supple line
or a beautiful flower. An abstraction invites an imitation.

– Conceiving an idea revolves around picking out a notion, a hazy
picture. First I work with graph paper as a kind of notebook. A rhythmic
play with squares and dots, full – open, heavy – light. To see the patterns
taking shape; a border, a star, a bird – creating fanciful ornaments. One
becomes fascinated by undreamed of possibilities and surprising
combinations. Then one experiments with needles and yarn to find a
colour palette. Test, choose, decide and change one's mind... follow an
idea from airy thinking through to an end which is a finished garment.

Simultaneously, one watches as time and tradition continue – stitch for
stitch, second for second – engendering a feeling of belonging and
continuity.

The shawl-collared sweater is knitted in the round to the neckline, with the armhole and neck steeks cut open afterwards.

SIZES
S (M) L (XL)

Total circumference: 40 (43) 45 3/4 (49)in
102 (109) 116 (124)cm

Total length: 25 1/4 (26 1/2) 27 (28 1/4)in
64 (67) 69 (72)cm

Underarm length: 20 (20 1/2) 21 (21 3/8)in
51 (52) 53 (54)cm

MATERIALS
Rauma Finull yarn (100% pure new wool) – 175 metres per 50 g) from Rauma Ullvarefabrikk:

black (436) 350 (350) 400 (450) g
red (499) 250 (300) 350 (400) g
green (484) 100 (100) 100 (150) g
orange (461) 100 (100) 100 (100) g
dark orange (434) 100 (100) 100 (100) g

Needles: circular and dpn 1 (2.5mm) and 2 (3mm).
Gauge/tension: 27 sts and 32 rows = 4 x 4in/10 x 10cm in pattern on ndls 2 (3mm)
Be sure that your gauge is correct! Change to larger or smaller ndls if necessary.

Pattern
Charts A–E show the body front and back, with D showing the front yoke and E the back yoke; chart F shows the entire sleeve. Sizes are marked on the charts with arrows and dark lines. Follow the arrows and lines marking your size.

Body
With black and ndl 1 (2.5mm), CO 252 (264) 276 (288) sts; join. Working in the round, knit 13 rnds for the facing; P 1 rnd for the turning and then work border A – begin at the arrow for your size on the right side and knit to the arrow for your size on the left side (= front). Then, begin at the arrow on the right side again and knit the sts for the back. On the last rnd of the border, inc to 274 (294) 314 (334) sts with the incs evenly spaced on the rnd. Place a marker at each side with 137 (147) 157 (167) sts between each marker. Change to ndl 2 (3mm) and work pattern B. Begin at the arrows for your size on the right side (both below and at the side of the chart); knit to the arrow on the left side; after the marker, begin again at the arrows on the right side and knit the sts for the back. At the arrow for the armhole, BO 1 st on each side of the marker on both sides. On the next rnd, CO 2 new sts over the bound-off sts and continue working in the round. The 2 new sts form the steek which is not worked in pattern. Purl the steek sts with both pattern yarns held together. BO 1 st at each side of the steek on every rnd 5 times. When pattern B is completed, knit border C. Then use pattern D for the front yoke and pattern E for the back yoke. At the arrow for the neckline, BO the centre 17 sts on the front. To avoid knitting back and forth, you can CO 3 new sts over the bound-off sts on the next row and continue knitting in the round. The steek sts are purled with both pattern yarns held together. Dec for the neck at each side of the steek – 1 st on every rnd 14 times.

At the arrow for the back neck, BO the centre 45 sts; work the rest of the body back and forth. Place the shoulder sts on a holder after completing the charted rows.

Sleeves
With black and dpn 1 (2.5mm), CO 54 (54) 54 (60) sts. Working in the round, knit 13 rnds for the facing and then purl 1 rnd for the turning. Continue working, following chart F between the arrows for your size. On the last rnd of the lower pattern border, inc to 69 (73) 77 (81) sts, with incs spaced evenly around. Change to ndl 2 (3mm) and continue working the main pattern. Inc 2 sts centred at the underarm every other rnd until you have 157 (167) 177 (187) sts on the ndl.
When the sleeve measures 18 1/2 (19) 19 1/4 (19 3/4)in/47 (48) 49 (50)cm (or 1 1/2 inches/4cm less than desired sleeve length), discontinue the main pattern. Work the top pattern border, with the last 7 rows of the border worked back and forth. When the pattern border is completed, work 8 rows in stockinette on the wrong side for the facing. BO.

Finishing
Machine-stitch 2 lines on each side of the centre of the steeks for the armholes and neck and cut between the lines. Weave the shoulder sts together.
Collar: Beginning at the lower left corner of the front neck opening, with black, larger ndls and right side facing, pick up and knit 12–13 sts for every 2in/5cm along the front, back, and down to the right corner of the front (do not pick up sts along the 17 bound-off sts). Work back and forth in twisted ribbing: K1 tbl, P1. After working 18 rows with black, work 1 row with dark orange. BO loosely with orange. Sew down both side edges of the collar against the 17 bound-off sts on the front for the shawl collar. Sew the underlying piece first. Sew the sleeves in and sew the lining over the cut edges on the wrong side.
Turn in all the facings and sew them loosely on the wrong side. Lightly steam the sweater.

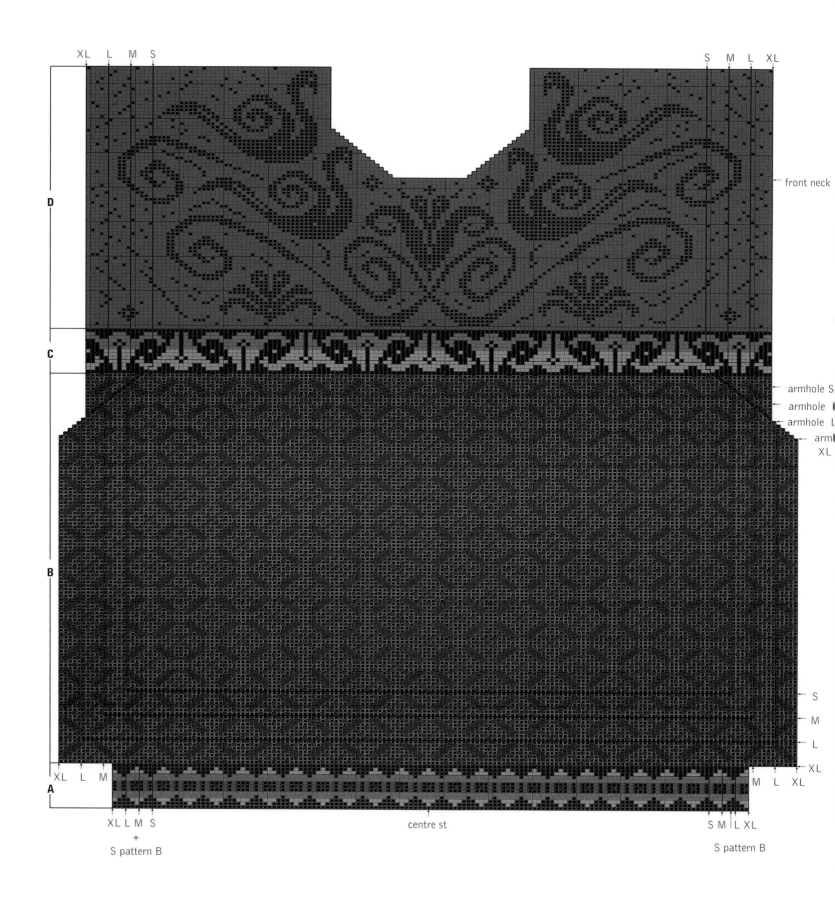

SVANEGENSER MED FUGLEMOTIV

SWAN SWEATER WITH BIRD MOTIFS

LISE KOLSTAD

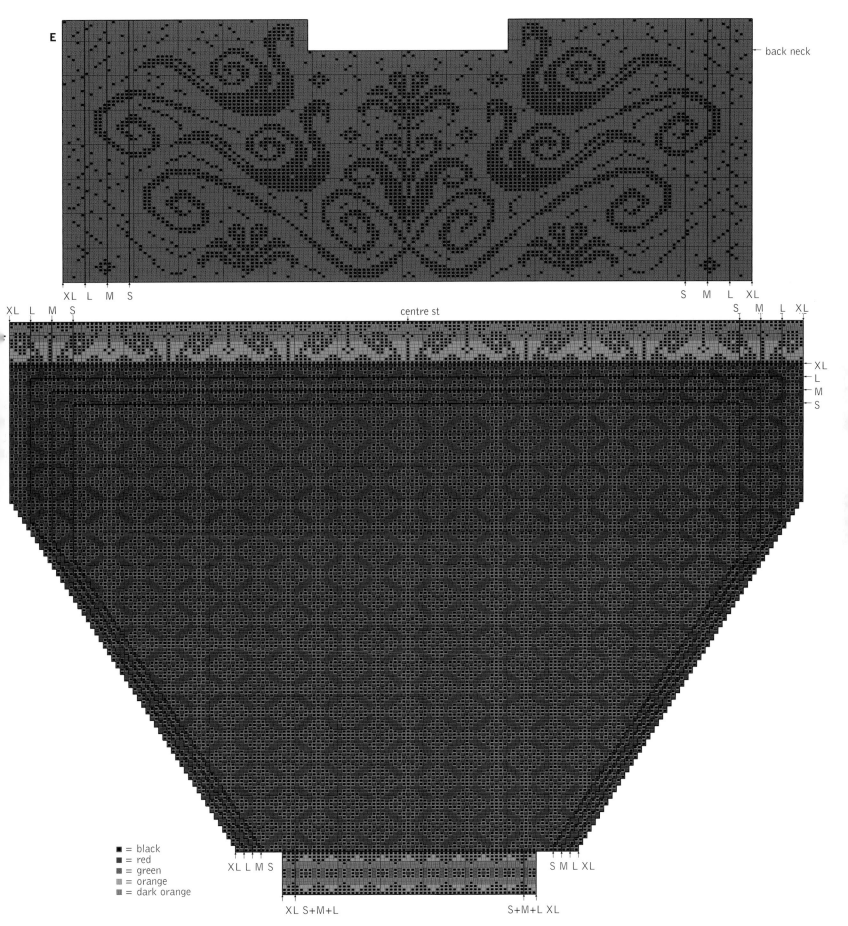

■ = black
■ = red
■ = green
■ = orange
■ = dark orange

EMBELLISHED JACKET WITH BIRDS

AND FLOWERS

The jacket is knitted in the round to the neck opening and then cut up the centre as are the armholes. The main pattern is knitted in two colours and the small dots of orange and red are later embroidered with duplicate stitch. A ruched edging is knitted around the front opening.

SIZES

S (M) L

Total circumference:	41 (43) 45 1/4in	
	104 (109) 115cm	
Total length:	21 3/4 (22 1/2) 23 1/2in	
	55 (57) 60cm	
Underarm length:	19 1/4 (20) 20 1/2in	
	49 (51) 52cm	

MATERIALS

Rauma Finull yarn (100% pure new wool – 175 metres per 50 g) from Rauma Ullvarefabrikk:

black (436)	300 (350) 400 g
light green (493)	250 (300) 350 g
green (430)	100 (100) 100 g
red (469)	100 (100) 100 g
orange (461)	50 (50) 50 g

Needles: circular and dpn 1 and 2 (2.5 and 3mm) + an extra long circular ndl 2 (3mm) for the ruched edging.

Notions/haberdashery: cotton bias tape to cover the raw edges on the inside of the front edgings and, if desired, hooks for the hidden front closure.

Be sure that your gauge is correct! Change to larger or smaller ndls if necessary.

Pattern

Charts A–C show the body front and back and chart D shows the entire sleeve. Sizes are marked on the charts with arrows and dark lines. Follow the arrows and lines marking your size.

Body

With red and ndls 1 (2.5mm), CO 250 (266) 282 sts; join. Working in the round, knit 1 1/2in/4cm for the facing. The first and last st on the rnd (2 sts) form the centre front steek and should always be purled. Knit an eyelet row for the turning: *K2 tog, yo*; repeat *–* around except over the steek sts (begin and end the rnd with K2tog on each side of the steek). Knit another 3 rnds with red. Place a marker at each side with 126 (134) 142 sts for the front (including the steek sts) and 123 (131) 139 sts for the back.

Knit border pattern A – begin after the steek sts with the centre st on the pattern and repeat the pattern repeat's 4 sts around. The steek is worked with both strands of the pattern yarns. Change to ndls 2 (3mm) and continue with border B and pattern C. Begin after the steek with the centre st on the pattern, knit to the arrow for your size on the left side (= right front). Continue after the marker at the arrow for your size at the right side and work across the pattern to the arrow for your size on the left side (= back). After the marker,

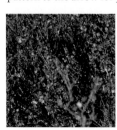

begin at the arrow on the right side again and knit to and including the centre st (= left front) + 2 steek sts. On every 5th rnd, inc 2 sts at each side (on each side of the markers) as shown on the pattern until you have a total of 281 (297) 313 sts on the ndl.

At the arrow marking the armhole, BO 6 sts at each side (3 sts on each side of the marker). On the next rnd, CO 2 new sts over the bound-off sts for the armhole steek. The steek sts are always purled with both strands of the pattern colours.

BO another 1 st on each side of the steek on every rnd, 2 times. At the arrow marking the neckline, BO the centre 18 sts on the front, including the steek sts, and finish the rnd. Cut yarn and begin the next row at the neck. Work back and forth. Continue with the neck decreases on each side on every row – 2 sts once and 1 st 7 times, then another 1 st on every alternate row 5 times.

At the arrow for the back neck, BO the centre 31 sts and work back and forth on each side separately. Dec at the neck edge on each row 2 sts twice and 1 st twice. Set the shoulder sts on a holder at the arrow for your size.

Sleeves

With red and ndls 1 (2.5mm), CO 52 (52) 56 sts; join. Work the facing and eyelet (turning) rnd as for the body. Continue with the pattern following chart D and working the sts between the arrows for your size. Change to ndls 2 (3mm) after the lower border is complete and, at the same time, inc to a total of 65 (71) 77 sts, with the inc sts evenly spaced around. Inc another 2 sts at the underarm every other rnd until you have 149 (161) 169 sts on the ndl. Knit to the arrow for your size, or to 1 1/2in/4cm before the desired length. Finish with the upper pattern border on all sizes, working the last 6 rnds of the border back and forth. Continue with light green and work 8 rows stockinette with the wrong side facing out for the facing. BO.

Finishing

Spread the pieces to the correct measurements, lay flat between damp towels, and leave until dry. Machine-stitch 2 lines on each side of the centre of the steeks for the armholes and centre front and cut between the lines. Weave the shoulder sts together. Turn the facings at the lower edges of the sleeves and body to the inside and sew them to the wrong side. Using duplicate st, embroider the little colour dots on the flowers on the body and sleeves.

Ruched edging: With red and ndls 2 (3mm), pick up and knit about 13 sts for every 2in/5cm. Beginning at the lower edge on the right front, continue around the neck and down the left front. The total number of sts should be divisible by 5 + 4 sts. Work 2 rows in stockinette, and then one row with «holes» as follows: *P3, P2tog, yo*; repeat *–* around to the last 4 sts; end P4. On the next row, knit all the sts but, in every yo, work 6 sts – alternating knit and purl sts. Knit one more row and BO.

Sew in the sleeves and sew the facings over the raw edges on the wrong side. Sew cotton bias tape over the raw edges on the inside of the jacket front. Lightly steam the jacket.

Sew hooks on the inside of the jacket edges if you wish.

PRYDJAKKE MED FUGLER OG BLOMSTER

EMBELLISHED JACKET WITH BIRDS

AND FLOWERS

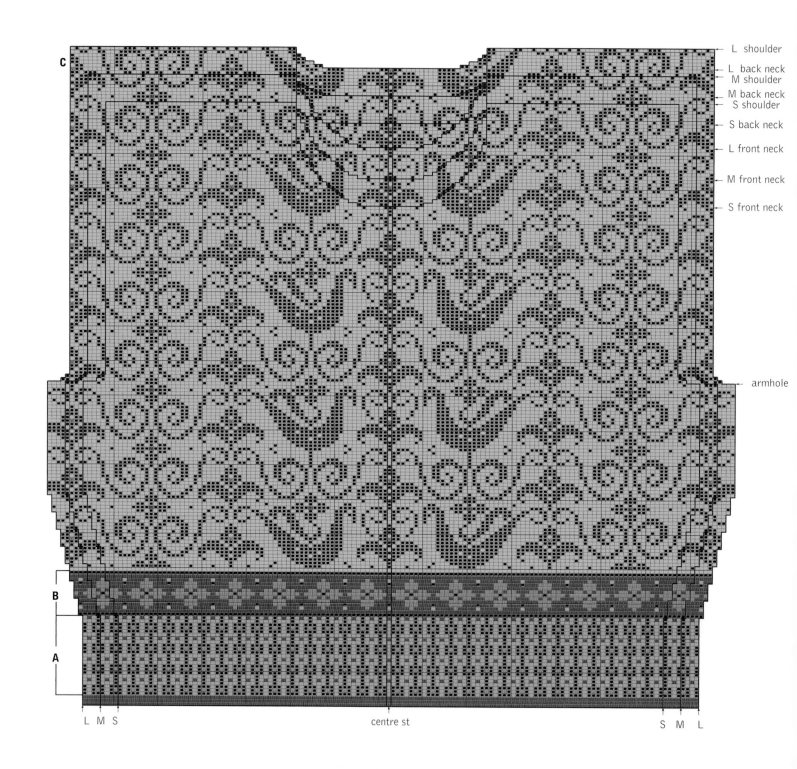

L shoulder
L back neck
M shoulder
M back neck
S shoulder
S back neck
L front neck
M front neck
S front neck

armhole

C

B

A

L M S

centre st

S M L

PRYDJAKKE MED FUGLER OG BLOMSTER

EMBELLISHED JACKET WITH BIRDS

AND FLOWERS

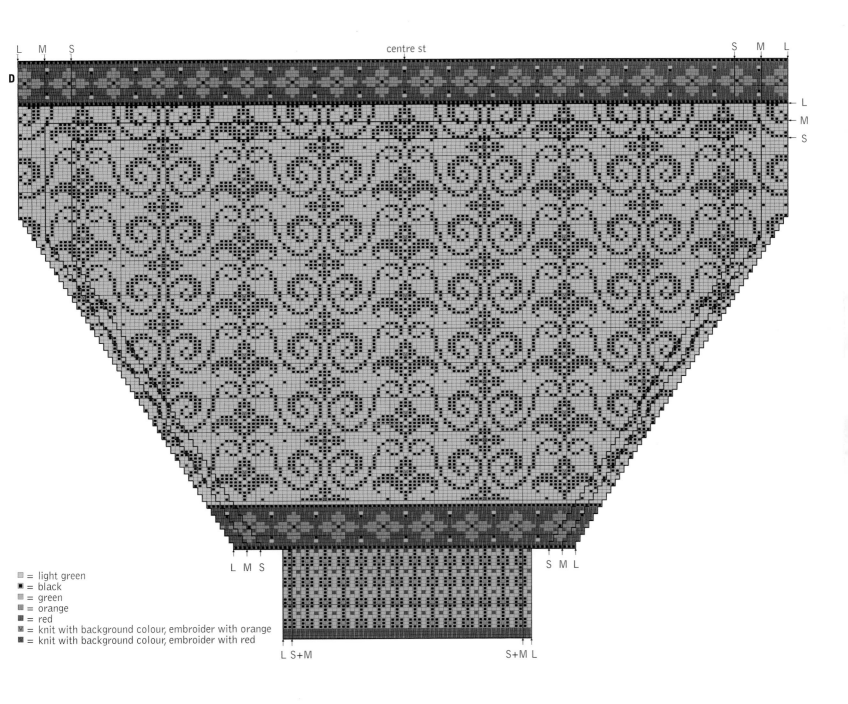

= light green
= black
= green
= orange
= red
= knit with background colour, embroider with orange
= knit with background colour, embroider with red

DESIGNER'S BACKGROUND AND INSPIRATION

A bride's bodice and
breast cloth from Hardanger

A chair found in an old house in
Rauland, Telemark

Solveig Hisdal
Born in 1946.

Education
Trained at the National Technical School for Art-Handicraft and Design
in Bergen and at the Fashion Institute of Technology in New York.

Publication
She wrote the book *Poetry in Stitches* in 1997. It has been translated
into several languages.

Awards
Solveig has won a number of awards for her designs. She has been
awarded the first prize in Norway's International Wool Secretariat's
Competition for Nordic Designers; the Mark for Good Design by the
Norwegian Design Council in 1993 and 1997 for Oleana and for
Irisfabrikken in 1998; Scheiblers Legat's Prize of Honor in 1995; and
the Silver Medal from the Royal Society for Norway's Welfare in 1998.

Exhibitions, Clothing
She has participated in a number of exhibits at home and abroad,
including: 'Moments of Norwegian Patterns' in Praha and Stockholm,
1991–92; Husfliden's Jubilee Exhibit 1991; 'Passion on Circular
Needles', travelling exhibit 1991–92; 'Organza and Taffeta', Gallery
Norwegian Form, Oslo 1992; 'I Discover, I Discover', Norwegian Folk
Museum, 1992; Women and Clothing Jubilee Exhibit, Oslo, 1993;
'Bridal Jackets from a City Maid', Hardanger Folk Museum, 1993;
'Form 96, Designer's Fall Exhibit' and 'Poetry in Stitches', Hardanger
Folk Museum and Drammen Museum 1997; 'Huldrestas', Horda
Museum 1997 and Arvika Art Gallery, Arvika, 1998.

Solveig's work (paintings) have been purchased by Hordaland County,
the Norwegian Culture Council, various institutions, and Vestland's Art
Industry Museum (clothing).

She is also known for her other design work which includes Oleana
products.

On designing
When I began designing knitwear, it was natural for me to go to
museums for inspiration. A visit to a museum's storerooms is like
entering paradise. It is mainly the old textiles which capture my interest.
These textiles offer me everything I could wish for – a wealth of old
clothing articles made from the most beautiful fabrics and in the most
wonderful colours and patterns which are lively and full of charm. The
surfaces of these fabrics were often embellished and decorated so one
finds many pretty pieces of handwork in these collections. When creating
a garment, I try to do more than just copy. I attempt to capture the
essence and mood of the old garments within today's styles.

GARTER STITCH JACKET, CAP AND BAG

The entire jacket is knitted from side to side in garter stitch. Identical colour stripes are worked on both the body and sleeves. Gussets are worked on the body's lower edge and under the sleeves so that the bodice curves inward. The cap and crocheted bag are decorated with glass beads.

SIZE
M

Total circumference:	37 1/2in/95cm
Width at the waist	33in/84cm
Total length:	24 1/4in/62cm
Underarm length:	18in/46cm

MATERIALS
Hifa 2 (100% pure new wool – 315 metres per 100 g) from Hillesvåg Ullvarefabrikk:
50 grams each:
dark burgundy (6072)
bungundy (6075)
dark rose (6018)
yellow (6094)
orange (6096)
dark orange (6003)
olive green (6090)
moss green (6109)
dark grey-blue (6104)
grey-blue (6037)
light blue (6081)
ecru (6107)
red (6013)
coral pink (6112)
100 grams coral (6111)
+100 grams red for the cap and 50 grams red for the bag.
Needles: straight or circular ndls 2 (3mm) for the jacket, a short circular needle and dpn 2 (3mm) for the cap, + crochet hook A (2mm).
Notions/haberdashery: black velvet and iron-on interfacing for the collar and, for example, floral-patterned cotton fabric for lining the collar and the bag, about 2 3/4 yds/2.5 m black velvet ribbon, 3/4in/2cm wide and 12 buttons. Glass beads for the cap and bag – here we've used red and green beads on the cap and rose, claret, red and green beads on the bag.
Gauge/tension: 21 sts and 23 ridges = 4 x 4in/10 x 10cm on ndls 2 (3mm).
Be sure that your gauge is correct! Change to larger or smaller needles if necessary.

STRIPE PATTERN
The whole jacket is knitted back and forth from side to side in garter stitch – knit every row (1 ridge = 2 rows). The following colour sequence is used for both the body and the sleeves.
Burgundy sequence: 1 ridge dark burgundy, 2 ridges burgundy, 1 ridge dark rose, 2 ridges burgundy and 1 ridge dark burgundy.
Yellow/green sequence: 1 ridge yellow, 1 ridge orange, 1 ridge dark orange, 1 ridge yellow, 1 ridge olive green, 1 ridge moss green, 1 ridge olive green, 1 ridge yellow and 1 ridge orange.
Blue sequence: 1 ridge dark grey-blue, 1 ridge grey-blue, 1 ridge light blue (= centre of the sequence), 1 ridge grey-blue and 1 ridge dark grey-blue.
Red sequence: 2 ridges ecru, 1 ridge coral, 1 ridge red, 1 ridge coral, 1 ridge coral pink, 2 ridges coral, 1 ridge red, 2 ridges coral, 1 ridge ecru, 1 ridge coral, 1 ridge coral pink, 1 ridge red (= centre of sequence), 1 ridge coral pink, 1 ridge coral, 1 ridge ecru, 2 ridges coral, 1 ridge red, 2 ridges coral, 1 ridge coral pink, 1 ridge coral, 1 ridge red, 1 ridge coral and 2 ridges ecru.

JACKET
Body
Knit following this colour sequence: 1 burgundy sequence, 1 yellow/green, 1 blue, 1 red (with the gusset at the lower edge), 1 blue (with both lower edge and sleeve gussets) 1 yellow/green – with reverse order of the colour stripes, 1 burgundy, 1 yellow/green (as for the first) 1 blue and 1 red (with the gusset at the lower edge) – this sequence marks the centre back.
With dark burgundy and ndls 2 (3mm), CO 115 sts for the left front. Knit the ridges in stripes and in the colour sequences as explained above, but begin with 3 ridges of dark burgundy. When you have a total of 14 ridges from the beginning, begin increasing for the neck: inc 1 st on each alternate row 7 times and then 7 sts once.
Shape the shoulders by binding off 1 st after the 10th ridge, and 1 st after the 20th ridge (the shoulders have 30 ridges altogether). However, for the centre ridge in the red sequence, make a gusset in the lower edge by knitting short rows in the following manner (the gusset is also worked in garter st): Knit 3 sts with red, turn and knit back, knit 8 sts with coral, turn and knit back. Continue knitting the ridges for the gusset alternating red and coral and knit 3 sts more every time you turn until you have 38 sts for the gusset (the last ridge is coral). Then knit with red the whole way up to the shoulder and down again (= the centre ridge in the red sequence). Knit the other half of the gusset in the same way, but in reverse order: begin with 38 sts with coral, turn and knit back, knit 35 sts with red, turn and knit back. Knit 3 sts fewer every time you turn until you have knitted over 8 sts with coral; knit the last ridge over 3 sts with red. Continue over all the sts, remembering to dec after 20 ridges for the shoulder.
When you have 30 ridges for the shoulder, BO for the armhole on each alternate row – 30 sts once and 5 sts 2 times. When you have knitted 16 ridges from the last gusset (the centre ridge is in the blue sequence), knit a gusset in the same way as the first one on the lower edge, but alternating light blue and grey-blue yarn. But, when half of the gusset is finished (last ridge = 38 sts with grey-blue), knit a half gusset from the armhole downwards. **NOTE:** The sts for the gusset must be purled on every row so that the stripes will be done correctly. The first ridge in the gusset is knitted with 4 sts with grey-blue, the next ridge over 8 sts with light blue. Continue knitting ridges, alternating grey-blue and light blue, and knit 4 sts more every time you turn – until you have 28 sts in the gusset (the last ridge with grey-blue). Knit 1 ridge with light blue over all the sts (= centre ridge in the blue sequence, centred under the armhole). Then finish the two gussets in the same manner, but in reverse order – at the lower edge begin with 38 sts grey-blue and knit 3 sts fewer each time you turn; at the armhole, begin with 28 sts grey-blue and knit 4 sts fewer each time you turn.
When the two gussets are finished, continue knitting over all the sts at the same time as you increase for the armhole on every second row – 5 sts 2 times and 30 sts once. When you have 10 ridges from the armhole, shape the shoulders by increasing 1 st here, and inc 1 st after the 20th ridge.
When you have 30 ridges on the shoulders (after 2 ecru ridges), begin the decreases for the neck: BO 1 st on every other row 4 times. Knit to the centre of the red sequence and make a gusset in the lower edge like the first one. This gusset is the centre back.
Continue knitting the other half of the body in the same manner, but in reverse order. Inc where you decreased and dec where you increased for the neck and armholes. On the yellow/green sequence knit the colour stripes in reverse order
When there are 4 ridges remaining to work, knit 10 buttonholes evenly spaced in the following manner from the lower edge and up: Knit 11 sts, BO 1 st, *K10, BO 1*; repeat from *–* until 4 sts remain, end K4. On the next row, CO 1 new st over each bound-off st. Finish with 3 ridges of dark burgundy and BO.

GARTER STITCH JACKET, CAP AND BAG

Sleeves

Work in the same order of colours and colour sequences – begin with 4 ridges of olive green, 1 ridge yellow, 1 ridge dark orange, 1 ridge orange and 1 ridge yellow. Then knit a burgundy sequence, 1 yellow/green sequence, 1 blue sequence and 1 red sequence – this marks the centre of the sleeve.

With olive green and ndls 2 (3mm), CO 8 sts. Knit 1 row. CO 5 new sts at the end of the row and continue knitting in garter st as explained above; at the same time, at the wrist inc 5 sts every other row until you have increased a total of 16 times; then inc 10 sts once. Also at the same time, when you have knitted 6 ridges from the cast-on row, begin increasing for the top of the sleeve: inc 1 st on every other row, 21 times and another 1 st every 4th row, 2 times. The centre ridge in the red colour sequence is the centre of the sleeve. Knit the other half, reversing the colour sequence.

Finishing

Weave in all ends neatly on the wrong side. Sew the shoulders together. Draw the pattern for the collar. Cut out the collar in the velvet and cotton fabrics, with the centre back against the edge of the fabric. Iron on interfacing and sew the collar together on the wrong side. Then stitch along the outer edge of the collar. Pin the velvet ribbon on each side of the front opening, and about 2in/5cm in along the neck opening on each side. Baste it first on the right side – the edge on the right side should be about 1/2in/1.5cm. Sew it by hand with small stitches. Turn 1/4in/0.5cm over the edge against the wrong side and sew it by hand. Sew the collar neatly around the neck opening and sew a velvet band or bias tape over the collar's raw edge on the wrong side. Sew on the buttons.

Sew the sleeve seams, but leave a 2 1/2in/6cm opening at the lower end for the slit.

Sew the velvet ribbon around the lower edge and along the slit opening. Make a button loop on one side of the slit and sew a button on the other side. Sew in the sleeves.

CAP

Pattern

The chart shows the pattern for the cap.

With red and ndls 2 (3mm), CO 112 sts. Work back and forth, knitting all rows (1 ridge = 2 rows). When you have completed 16 ridges, change to knitting in the round and work the pattern following the chart – repeat the section from *–* around. After completing the charted rows, work garter st in the round: alternate knit and purl rows. At the same time, decrease as follows: *K5, K2tog; repeat from * around. Work 3 rnds without decreasing. On the next

rnd, *K4, K2tog; repeat from * around. Decrease in the same manner every 4th rnd, but with 1 less st between the decreases on each dec rnd. Work until 32 sts remain. Work 1 rnd without decreasing, and then K2, K2tog around. Cut yarn and draw it through the rest of the sts and weave in the end on the wrong side. Sew the ridge edge together at the centre back. Crochet 1 rnd dc around the lower edge – with 2 dc in every st around. Finish with a picot edge in the following manner: 1 sc through the back loop of the dc, *3 chain sts, 1 dc in the first of the 3 chain sts, skip over 3 sts, 1 sc through the back loop of the next dc; repeat from * around, finishing with 1 slip st the first st. Sew on the beads.

CROCHETED BAG

Make a small ring with the yarn and work 6 sc in the ring; join the ring with the end of the yarn. Continue working in a spiral, with sc through the back loops.

2nd rnd: 2 sc in each st around = 12 sc.

3rd–15th rnds: Inc 4 sts evenly spaced on each rnd = 64 sc on the 15th round. Continue working without any further increases until the bag measures about 8in/20cm.

Crochet an eyelet row for the drawstring as follows: Begin with 2 chain st (= 1 dc), 2 dc, * 2 ch, skip 2 sts, 3 dc; repeat from * around, finishing with 2 ch sts. Continue crocheting 2 rnds with chain st loops: begin with slip sts to the centre of the first loop, * 5 ch, 1 sc in the next loop; repeat from * around. Finish with 5 sc in every loop around. Twist two 20–24in/50–60cm long drawstrings. Pull the drawstrings through the loops. Attach beaded tassels to the ends of the drawstrings and at the bottom of the bag. Sew beads onto the bag and line it with fabric.

■ = knit
■ = purl

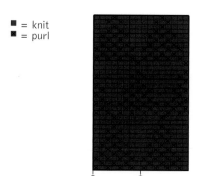

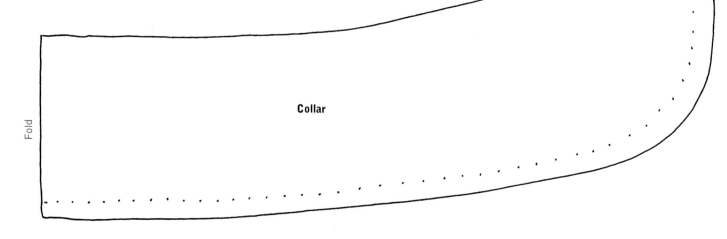

Fold

Collar

JACKET

The jacket is knitted in the round to the armholes and then worked back and forth. It is later cut up the centre front. The ends of the sleeves are knitted with garter stitch ridges and then finished with crocheted ruches.

SIZES
S (M) L
Total circumference: 45 1/2 (50 1/2) 52 3/4in
116 (128) 134cm
Total length: 26 3/4 (28) 28 3/4in
68 (71) 73cm
Underarm length: 17 3/4 (17 3/4) 17 3/4in
45 (45) 45cm

MATERIALS
Heimly (100% pure new wool – 120 metres per 50 g) from SandnesGarn:
off-white (131)   450 (500) 550 g
light blue (342)   200 (200) 250 g
blue (357)   100 (100) 100 g
mustard yellow (450)   100 (100) 100 g
red (257)   50 (50) 50 g
Needles: circular and dpn 1 (2.5mm) and 2 (3mm), plus crochet hook A (2mm).
Notions/haberdashery: 7 buttons
Gauge/tension: 26 sts and 32 rows in colour pattern, 38 rows in one colour with purl st pattern on ndl 2 (3mm) = 4 x 4in/10 x 10cm.
Be sure that your gauge is correct! Change to larger or smaller needles if necessary.

PATTERN
Chart A shows the body front and back and chart B shows the entire sleeve. All sizes are marked on the charts with arrows and dark lines. Follow the arrows and marking lines for your size.

Body
With off-white and ndls 1 (2.5mm), CO 315 (347) 363 sts. Working back and forth in stockinette (the first row is the wrong side), work 12 rows in off-white and 2 rows red for the facing. Change to ndls 2 (3mm) and knit one row on the wrong side for the turning row. CO 4 new sts at the centre front for the steek; join and continue in stockinette, knitting in the round. The steek sts are always purled without any patterning throughout. Knit 3 rnds red and then continue, following the pattern on chart A: after the steek sts, begin at the arrow for the right front and knit to the arrow for your size on the left side and place a marker in the last st (= side st). Beginning at the arrow on the right side, knit the whole pattern to the arrow on the left side and place a marker in the last st (= side st). Beginning at the arrow for your size at the right side again, knit to the arrow indicating the end of the left front. Dec 1 st on each side of the side sts 5 times as indicated on the chart. At the arrow for the armhole, BO 7 sts on each side. Finish the rnd and cut yarn. Continue, working back and forth and working the back and fronts separately. Begin the row at the armhole.
Front: Continue with armhole decs, at the beginning of each row, at each side, dec 2-2 sts.
At the arrow for the neckline, BO the 4 steek sts + 7 (8) 9 sts at each side and work each side separately. At the neck edge, dec at the beginning of each row 3-2-2 sts and 1 st 5 times.
Shape the shoulders by setting aside sts at the armhole edge, every other row, as shown on the chart.
Back: Dec for the armhole as for the fronts. BO the centre 35 (37) 39 sts for the neck at the same time as you shape the shoulders. Work each side of the neck separately. Continue decreasing at the beginning of each row for the neck 2-2 sts.

Sleeves
With red and ndls 1 (2.5mm), CO 56 (62) 68 sts. Working back and forth, knit in garter st (knit every row; 1 ridge = 2 rows). Knit 2 ridges with red and 8 ridges with off-white. Change to ndls 2 (3mm) and begin working in the round, following chart B and working the sts between the arrows for your size. The first st on each row is the centre st of the underarm. Inc 1 st on each side of that centre st every 4th rnd until you have a total of 118 (124) 130 sts on the ndl. When the sleeve is about 17 3/4in/45cm long or desired length to underarm, BO 7 sts centred at the underarm and continue, working back and forth. At the beginning of every row at each side, dec 2 sts twice and then BO the rest of the sts on a right side row.

Finishing
Machine-stitch two lines on each side of the centre of the front steeks on the body and cut between the lines. Knit the shoulders together.
Front bands: with off-white and ndls 1 (2.5mm), pick up and knit 154 (166) 172 sts along the left front (about 13 sts for every 2in/5cm). Knit 1 row on the wrong side and then 8 rows stockinette. At the same time, on every other row, inc 1 st before the 2nd to the last st at the neck opening. Change to mustard yellow and work 4 rows stockinette and dec 1 st before last st at the neck opening on the last row. Change to off-white and continue in stockinette and dec 1 st at the neck on every other row. After 12 rows in off-white have been worked, BO all sts.
Pick up and knit a corresponding edge along the right front, but, on the 5th row of stockinette, make 7 buttonholes evenly spaced on the edging – the lowest 18 sts from the lower edge and the rest with 19 (21) 22 sts in-between. BO 3 sts for every buttonhole and CO 3 new sts over each buttonhole on the next row. Make corresponding buttonholes on the 5th row of the facing with off-white.

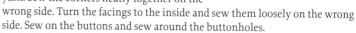

Neckband: With off-white and ndl 1 (2.5mm), pick up and knit about 131 (135) 139 sts around the neck opening. Work in the same way as for the front bands, but inc and dec at each end (at the centre front), and change to red instead of yellow yarn. Sew the corners neatly together on the wrong side. Turn the facings to the inside and sew them loosely on the wrong side. Sew on the buttons and sew around the buttonholes.
Ruched edgings: Sew the ridged rows together at the lower edge of the sleeve and crochet ruches as follows: Begin in the topmost white ridge. Hold the sleeve with the lower edge towards you and crochet 1 rnd of dc with off-white – (2 dc in one st, 1 dc in each of the next 2 sts) around, finishing with 1 slip st. Turn work upside down and crochet 1 rnd sc with mustard yellow, through the back loops from the wrong side of the dc – (2 sc in one st, 1 sc in the next st) around, finishing with 1 slip st. *Skip over 1 ridge; crochet a similar ruche in the next ridge. Repeat from * a total of 3 times, but, in the last ruche, work the sc row with red instead of yellow. Finish by crocheting 1 rnd dc in the cast-on row. Hold the sleeve at the lower edge in front of you and crochet with red – 2 dc in each st around; finish with 1 slip st. Sew in the sleeves.

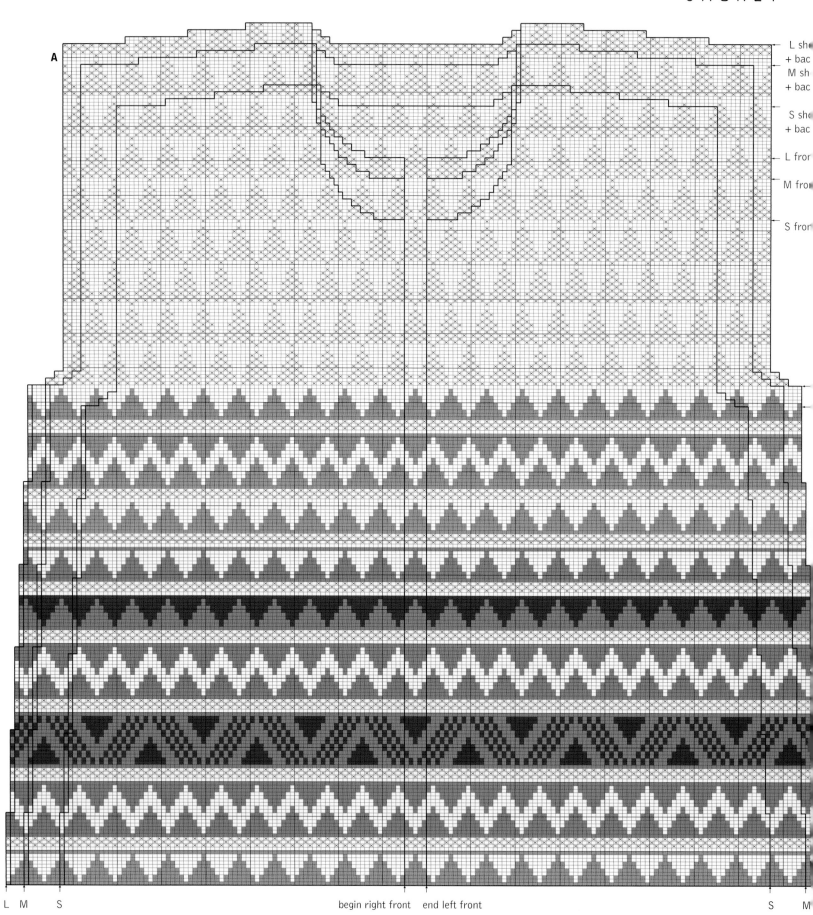

A

L sh
+ bac

M sh
+ bac

S sh
+ bac

L fron

M fron

S fron

L   M   S   begin right front   end left front   S   M

JAKKE

JACKET

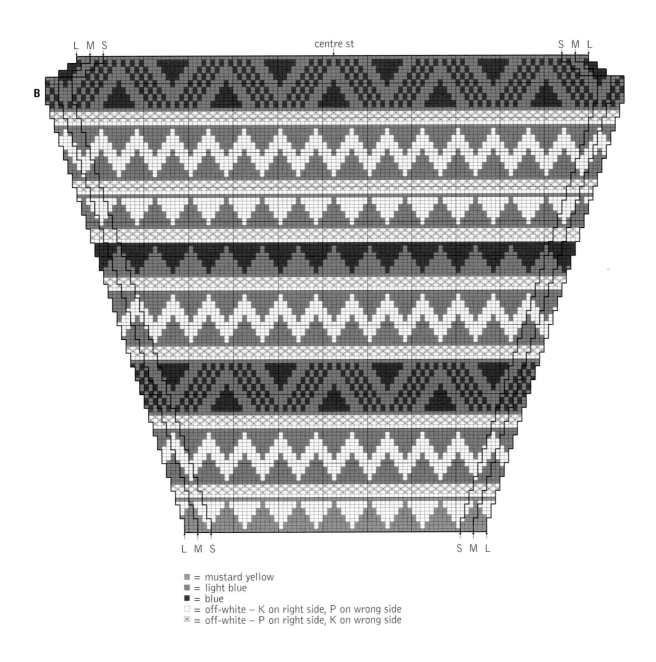

☐ = mustard yellow
☐ = light blue
■ = blue
☐ = off-white – K on right side, P on wrong side
☒ = off-white – P on right side, K on wrong side

DESIGNER'S BACKGROUND AND INSPIRATION

Kirsti Bræin
Born in 1960.

Education
Trained at the National Handicraft and Art-Industry School, Institute for Clothing and with IFM Westerdals, layout and typography.

Scholarships
National 3-year work scholarship for artists 1997–99, US.-Norway Fulbright Foundation Scholarship, 1995–96; Johnsson's Legacy 1995; National travel or study scholarship 1991 and National start-up scholarship 1989.

Professional Work
Kirsti has designed for and worked with knitwear manufacturers and yarn companies since 1984.
She has been a Visiting Lecturer and Examiner at the Institute for Clothing and Costume with SHKS since 1990.
In 1988, she and Iselin Hafseld established the trademark NORI Design, which produces both manufactured and handmade knitted and sewn clothing. She had her own shop from 1988 until 1992. NORI's collections have been displayed at fashion shows in Düsseldorf, Germany as well as at several venues in Norway. NORI's clothing has been sold in Scandinavia and Germany. The choreographer Kjersti Alveberg commissioned knitted outfits from NORI for the closing ceremonies at the Olympics in Albertville in 1992.
In 1995–96, she pursued research on historical clothing and textiles (U.S.- Norway Fulbright Foundation Scholarship), primarily at the Metropolitan Museum of Art and The Costume Collection of the Fashion Institute of Technology in New York City, USA. In the fall of 1996, she worked with the Metropolitan Opera, Costume Department. She established her own clothing and textile workshop in Oslo in 1997.

Awards
1990: first prize, Official World Cup sweater, 'Fiemme', for The Norwegian Ski team, produced by Dale of Norway.
1991: Norwegian Form's Annual Prize for Creativity and New Thinking to NORI.
Prize for Official Olympic sweater 'Albertville', for The Norwegian Olympic team, produced by Dale of Norway.

Exhibitions
Kirsti has participated in a number of exhibitions in Norway and abroad, including:
'Glowing Colours and Glistening Gold', Art-Industry Museum in Oslo, 1998 – a collaboration with the textile artist, Jorun Schumann, for clothing design with her fabrics for the solo exhibition, 'Draperies' at RAM Gallery, Oslo, 1998.
'Point Exhibit Knitting', Kent State University Museum, Ohio, USA, 1996; 'Norwegian Days in Malmö and Lund', Malmö, 1996, arranged by the Royal Norwegian Ambassador; 'Breaking', Nordenfjeldske Art-Industry Museum, Trondheim, 1995; 'Norwegian Art-Handicraft', Bodø Art Association, 1994; 'Troll Straw and Old Women Spinning, Maihaugen, Lillehammer, 1993–94; 'Moments of Norwegian Pattern', Praha, 1992; 'Knitting Norwegian', Stockholm, 1992; 'Passion on Circular Needles', travelling exhibit, Maihaugen, Lillehammer, 1991–92; 'Bare in Blue', Gallery Vognremissen, Oslo, 1991; 'Crossing Point', Høvikodden, 1991; 'Clothing and Jewelry 89', Gallery Karl Johan, Oslo, 1989; 'Tomorrow's Heirlooms', The Norwegian Theater, Oslo, 1989.

Kirsti's designs have been purchased by the Art-Industry Museum in Oslo and the National Institute of Fashion Technology, New Delhi, India.

On Designing
When I create clothing, whether knitted or with other materials, I am always concerned with the totality of the cloth. These are the elements of form, colour use and ornament. In working with knitting, all of these elements are important. I first let the yarn quality and colours give me an immediate idea about what I'd like to create.
I find inspiration for my work in my experiences.
That can be in art, nature, colours, music. I find inspiration in historic and contemporary materials and in pictures, books, photographs and objects – one can see impulses for new ideas everywhere.

– For me, to use inspiration means to form associations and impressions from a starting point through to the material I desire. I've developed my ideas for sweaters in Finull from Rauma in that way (see 'Princess-Line Sweater' on pages 50–53). Here the jumping-off point and inspiration is a bridal crown from Sunnmøre. I had wanted to convey and refashion it for knitting, retaining the essences of the gilded bridal crown's form and ornament. I have reproduced the crown's form in the sweater's curving lines and recreated the decorations on the crown in the sweater's ornamentation.

– The starting point for the piece with Peer Gynt yarn from Sandnes Garn (see 'Sweater with Detached Collar, Cap and Wristwarmers' on pages 46–49) was found in one of Karl Blossfeldt's plant photos – nature's organic forms. To portray this idea, I developed the ornamentation from a little textile sample in single-colour jacquard, which I found in a textile collection at the Fashion Institute of Technology in New York City. This little detail had something which I associated with the photograph.

– In the two garments I present in this book, I have chosen to differentiate style and inspiration, although they are related through the blue colours in both models which bind them together.
In my two sweaters, the ornamentation relates something of the style and inspiration while, simultaneously, the colours are used to paint a difference.

SWEATER WITH DETACHED COLLAR, CAP AND WRISTWARMERS

The sweater is knitted in the round up to the shoulders and then cut open for the neckline and armholes.

SIZES

S/M (M/L)

Total circumference:	47 1/2 (49 1/4)in	121 (125)cm
Total length:	21 1/4 (23 1/2in	54 (60)cm
Sleeve length:	19 (19 1/4)in	48 (49)cm

MATERIALS

Peer Gynt (100% pure new wool – 91 metres per 50 g) from SandnesGarn:

black (18)	600 (650) g
blue (381)	200 (250) g
green (298)	150 (200) g
red-brown (234)	100 (100) g
grey-blue (525)	100 (100) g
light brown tweed (228)	50 (50) g
brown tweed (230)	50 (50) g

+ 200 g blue (381) for the cap and wristwarmers

Needles: circular ndl and dpn 4 (3.5mm).

Notions/haberdashery: 4 buttons for the detached collar.

Gauge/tension: 21 sts and 26 rows = 4 x 4in/10 x 10cm in stockinette and pattern.

Be sure that your gauge is correct! Change to larger or smaller needles if necessary.

SWEATER

Pattern

Chart A shows the body front and back; chart B shows the entire sleeve. Sizes are marked on the body with arrows and dark lines. Follow the arrows and lines marking your size. The parts of the chart with white background colour are not used for the sizes in this pattern but show how the pattern can be widened.

Body

With black and ndl 4 (3.5mm), CO 244 (248) sts; join. Working in the round, rib K2, P2 for 1 5/8 (2)in/4 (5)cm. Next, purl 1 rnd. Place a marker at each side, with 122 (124) sts in between each for the front and back pieces. Continue with the pattern, following chart A: Beginning at the arrow for your size on the right side, knit to the arrow on the left side = front. Beginning at the arrow on the right side again after the marker, knit the sts for the back in the same way. **NOTE:** The pattern is knitted in stockinette except for rnds 2, 5, and 8 which are K1, P1 ribbing. Inc 1 st on each side of the markers (= 4 inc per rnd). For size S/M: inc on rnd 25 and then every 16th rnd 2 times; size M/L: inc on rnd 18 and then every 15th rnd 3 times = 256 (264) sts. Continue, following the chart for the entire length. Finish the pattern at the arrow for your size and, continuing with black only, knit 1 rnd and then work in K2, P2 ribbing for 3/4 (1 1/8)in/2 (3)cm. BO.

Sleeves

With black and ndls 4 (3.5mm), CO 68 (68) sts. Work K2, P2 ribbing for 3/4 (1 1/8)in/2 (3)cm on on the body. Next, purl 1 rnd. Continue in pattern, following chart B. **NOTE:** The pattern is knitted in stockinette except for rnds 2, 5, and 8 which are K1, P1 ribbing. Inc 2 sts centred at the underarm as shown on the chart (the incs are the same for both sizes). Finish the pattern when the sleeve measures about 19 (19 1/4)in/48 (49)cm. Continue with black only – knit 1 rnd and then knit the facing, working back and forth – work 5 rows stockinette with the wrong side facing out. BO.

Finishing

Lightly steam the pieces on the wrong side. Baste a line for the neckline in an even arc – it should be about 2 3/4 (3)in/ 7 (7.5) cm deep at the centre of the front, 3/4in/2cm deep at the centre of the back and 9 (9 1/2)in/23 (24)cm wide. Be sure that the rest of the sts for the shoulders are even on each side. Machine-stitch just inside the basting thread and then sew a zigzag line just inside the seam. Wait to cut the neck opening until the neckband has been knitted! Mark the width for the sleeves at each side from the shoulders downwards and baste. Machine-stitch two lines on each side of the basting thread, a straight line then a zigzag and cut between them. Sew the shoulders together. Sew the sleeves in from the wrong side, using backstitch. Turn the facing over the raw edges and sew it loosely on the wrong side.

Neckband: with black and ndls 4 (3.5mm), pick up and knit 106 (110) sts around the neck opening. Purl 2 rnds. Change to red-brown and *knit 1 rnd, then 1 rnd of K1, P1 ribbing. At the same time, BO 1 st at each side of the shoulder seam (= 4 sts bound-off on the rnd). Then knit 1 rnd with black. Repeat from * 2 times more, but knit the colour stripe 1 time with grey-blue and 2 times with blue.

Continue with black only and knit 2 rnds; purl 1 rnd for the turning and then work 9 rnds in stockinette for the facing. At the same time, inc 1 st on each side of the shoulder seams (= 4 increased sts on the rnd) on every other rnd, 3 times. BO loosely.

Cut the neck opening neatly and then turn the facing in and sew it loosely over the cut edge on the wrong side. Carefully steam on the wrong side with a damp cloth over the neckband and sleeve facings.

DETACHED COLLAR

Pattern

Chart C shows the pattern for the collar

With black and ndls 4 (3.5mm), CO 124 sts. Working back and forth, rib 4 rows as follows: 1st row (= wrong side): P3, *K2, P2; repeat from * around, ending with P3. Work 3 more rows, knitting over the knit sts and purling the purl sts. Next, knit 1 row on the wrong side, decreasing to 102 sts with the decs spaced evenly across the row. Change to blue, knit 1 row, then work 1 row in K1, P1 ribbing. Continue, working back and forth and following the pattern on chart C. The first and last sts of each row are worked with both colours held together and are not worked in pattern. When you've completed all the charted rows, continue with blue – knit 1 row, then work 1 row in K1, P1 ribbing. Finish by knitting 1 row in black and then binding off.

With black and ndls 4 (3.5mm), pick up and knit 54 sts along the right side of the detached collar. Work 1 5/8in/4cm in K2, P2 ribbing. BO in ribbing. Work the same edging on the left side of the collar, but, after 3/4in/2cm, work 4 buttonholes evenly spaced along the row. BO 2 sts for each buttonhole and, on the next row, CO 2 new sts over the bound-off sts. Weave in all ends on the wrong side and steam the collar on the wrong side. Sew on the buttons.

WRISTWARMERS

With blue and dpn 4 (3.5mm), CO 44 sts; join. Work K2, P2 ribbing in the round, in for 8 3/4in/22cm. BO loosely in ribbing. Knit the other ristwarmer in the same way. Carefully steam on the wrong side under a damp cloth.

SWEATER WITH DETACHED COLLAR, CAP

AND WRISTWARMERS

CAP

With blue and dpn 4 (3.5mm), CO 120 sts; join. Working in the round, knit 4 rnds in stockinette for the facing; purl 1 rnd for the turning, and then knit 3 rnds in stockinette. On the last rnd, inc 40 sts evenly spaced around = 160 sts. Begin the cables:

Rnds 1–3: *K8, P2; repeat from * around.

Rnd 4: *Place 4 sts on a cable ndl behind the work, K4, then knit the sts from the cable ndl, P2; repeat from * around.

Rnds 5–13: *K8, P2; repeat from * around.

Rnd 14: same as rnd 4.

Rnds 15–23: same as rnds 5–13.

Rnd 24: same as rnd 4.

Rnds 25–31: same as rnds 5–13.

Rnd 32: *K1, K2tog, K2, K2tog, K1, P2; repeat from * around.

Rnd 33: *Place 3 sts on a cable ndl behind the work, K3, then knit the sts from the cable ndl, P2; repeat from * around.

Rnds 34–39: *K6, P2; repeat from * around.

Rnd 40: same as rnd 33.

Rnds 41–44: Same as rnds 34–39.

Rnd 45: *K1, K2tog, K2tog, K1, P2; repeat from * around.

Rnd 46: Place 2 sts on the cable ndl behind the work, K2, then knit the sts from the cable ndl, P2; repeat from * around.

Rnds 47–50: *K4, P2; repeat from * around.

Rnd 51: same as rnd 46.

Rnds 52–53: same as rnds 47–50.

Rnd 54: *K2tog, K2tog, P2; repeat from * around.

Rnd 55: *Place 1 st on the cable ndl behind the work, K1, then knit the st from the cable ndl, P2; repeat from * around.

Rnds 56–57: *K2, P2; repeat from * around.

Rnd 58: same as rnd 55.

Rnd 59: *K2, P2tog; repeat from * around.

Rnd 60: *K2, P1; repeat from * around.

Rnd 61: *Place 1 st on the cable ndl behind the work, knit 1 st and then knit the st from the cable ndl, P1; repeat from * around.

Rnd 62: same as rnd 60.

Rnd 63: *K2tog, P1; repeat from * around.

Rnd 64: *K1, P1; repeat from * around.

Rnd 65: *K2, K2tog; repeat from * around.

Rnd 66: Knit around.

Rnd 67: same as rnd 65.

Rnds 68–69: Knit around.

Cut yarn and bring through the remaining sts; weave in neatly on the wrong side.

Turn the facing to the inside and sew it loosely on the wrong side.

Lightly steam the cap on the wrong side under a damp cloth.

SWEATER WITH DETACHED COLLAR, CAP AND WRISTWARMERS

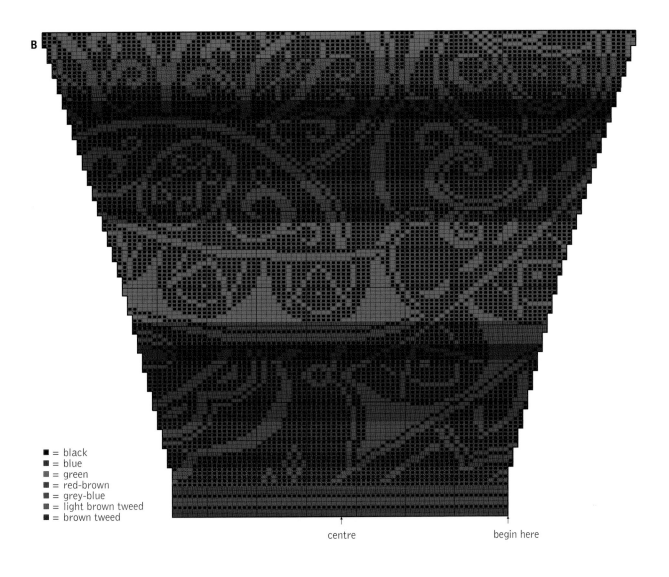

■ = black
■ = blue
■ = green
■ = red-brown
■ = grey-blue
■ = light brown tweed
■ = brown tweed

centre

begin here

begin here

49

PRINCESS-LINE SWEATER

The sweater is knitted in the round up to the shoulders, and then cut open for the neck and armholes. The pattern can be knitted in two colours and the details in other colours can be embroidered in later with duplicate stitch.

SIZES

S/M (M/L)

Total circumference:	44 (45 3/4) inches	112 (116)cm
Total length:	21 1/4 (23) inches	54 (58)cm
Sleeve length:	19 (19 1/4) inches	48 (49)cm

MATERIALS

Rauma Finull yarn (100% pure new wool about 175 metres per 50 g) from Rauma Ullvarefabrikk:

black (436)	350 (400) g
blue (467)	300 (350) g
turquoise (484)	50 (50) g
olive (476)	50 (50) g
brown (422)	50 (50) g
red-brown (423)	50 (50) g

Needles: circular and dpn 2 (3mm).
Gauge/tension: 26 sts and 32 rows = 4 x 4 in/10 x 10cm in stockinette st and pattern.
Be sure that your gauge is correct! Change to larger or smaller needles if necessary.

PATTERN

Chart A shows the body front and back; chart B shows the entire sleeve. On the body, the sizes are marked with arrows and dark lines. Follow the arrows and marking lines for your size. The parts of the chart with white background colour are not used for the sizes in this pattern but show how the pattern can be widened.

Body

With black and circular ndl 2 (3mm), CO 300 (308) sts; join. Working in the round, rib K2, P2 in the following colour sequence: 1 (1) rnd black, 3 (4) rnds blue, 2 (2) rnds brown, 2 (2) red-brown, 2 (2) turquoise, 8 (12) blue, and 2 (2) rnds black. Then knit 1 rnd with black and, at the same time, dec to 274 (282) sts with decs spaced evenly around. Place a marker at each side, with 137 (141) sts each for the front and back. Continue, following chart A for the pattern: K1 st blue (= side st); beginning at the arrow for your size on the right side, knit to the arrow on the left side (= front), K2 blue (= side st). Beginning at the arrow on the right side again, knit the sts for the back, ending with 1 st blue (= side st). The 2 blue sts on each side are always knitted with blue and not worked in pattern for the entire length. Dec 1 st at each side of the side sts (= 4 decs per rnd) on every 4th (3rd) rnd and then every 3rd rnd 10 times, then once after 3 rnds and finally once after 4 rnds = 222 (230) sts for the waist. Knit 5 rnds after the last dec and then begin increasing. Inc 1 st on each side of the side sts on the next rnd, then every 3rd rnd 3 times and, finally, every alternate rnd 14 (15) times = 294 (306) sts for the chest. Continue following the pattern on the chart until the total length is reached. BO in knitting for the shoulders at the arrows for your size.

Sleeves

With black and dpn 2 (3mm), CO 88 (88) sts; join. Working in the round, rib K2, P2 in the following colour sequence: 1 (1) rnd black, 3 (4) rnds blue, 2 (2) rnds brown, 2 (2) rnds red-brown, 2 (2) rnds turquoise, 6 (9) rnds blue, 2 (2)

rnds black. Then knit 1 rnd with black and, at the same, dec to 83 (83) sts with the decs spaced evenly around. Continue, working the pattern on chart B, with 2 blue sts centred at the underarm and not worked in pattern. Inc 1 st at each side of the 2 blue underarm sts as shown on the chart (the same for both sizes). Finish the pattern when the total length measures about 19 (19 1/4)in/48 (49)cm. Continuing with black, knit 1 rnd then begin working back and forth. For the facing, work 6 rows in stockinette with the wrong side facing out. BO.

Finishing

Lightly steam the pieces on the wrong side. Baste a line for the neckline in an even arc – it should be about 2 3/4 (3)in/ 7 (7.5cm) deep at the centre of the front, 3/4in/2cm deep at the centre of the back and 9 (9 1/2)in/23 (24)cm wide. Be sure that the rest of the sts for the shoulders are even on each side. Machine-stitch just inside the basting thread and then sew a zigzag line just inside the seam. Wait to cut the neck opening until the neckband has been knitted! Mark the width for the sleeves at each side from the shoulders downwards and baste. Machine-stitch two lines on each side of the basting thread, a straight line, then a zigzag and cut between them. Use duplicate stitch to embroider the details at the centre of the front, and on the back and sleeves as shown on the chart. Sew the shoulders together. Sew in the sleeves on the wrong side, using backstitch. Turn the facing to the inside over the raw edges and sew it loosely on the wrong side.

Neckband: With blue and circular ndl 2 (3mm), pick up and knit 124 (128) sts; join. Working in stockinette, knit 1 rnd with black and, at the same time, dec 1 st on each side of the shoulder seams (= 4 sts decreased on a rnd). Dec in the same manner on every other rnd another 3 times, knitting in the following colour sequence: 1 rnd blue, 1 rnd brown, 1 rnd red-brown, 1 rnd turquoise and 2 rnds blue. Continue with blue in K2, P2 ribbing until the neckband measures a total of 4in/10cm. However, when the band measures about 2 3/4in/7cm, inc 2 sts at each shoulder seam every other rnd, 4 times. BO loosely. Neatly cut the neck opening, turn the neckband in half to the wrong side and sew it loosely over the raw edges. Lightly steam the whole sweater under a damp cloth.

PRINCESS-LINE SWEATER

■ = black
■ = blue
■ = turquoise
■ = duplicate st embroidery with turquoise
■ = duplicate st embroidery with olive
■ = duplicate st embroidery with brown
■ = duplicate st embroidery with red-brown

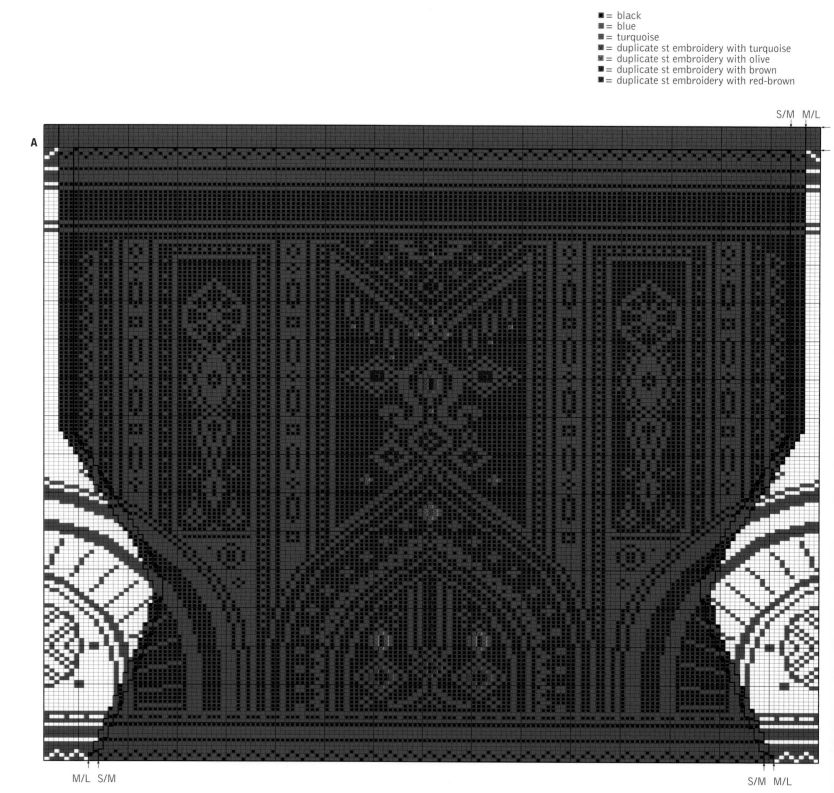

S/M M/L

A

M/L S/M

S/M M/L

PRINCESS-LINE SWEATER

B

begin here

DESIGNER'S BACKGROUND AND INSPIRATION

Kari Hestnes
Born in Trondheim in 1959.

Education
Trained in several fields, including sewing, weaving, furniture-making, drawing, form, and colour.

Publications
Kari Hestnes has written many books, including Knitting from T*radition to Fashion* and *Knit in Your Colours*. her latest book is *Knitting Poetry* (2017).

Professional Work
Kari Hestnes has worked as a knit designer since the eighties, and many of her designs are inspired by Frieda Kahlo. She is a co-owner of the company Du Store Alpakka, one of the largest importers of alpaca yarns in Norway. She regularly provides many knitting patterns for magazines.

On Designing
– I have worked with knitting design for the past 15 years and, for me, it is first and foremost the handwork that appeals to me. I lack the ability to visualize pictures and therefore cannot 'see' a design in my mind's eye. For that reason, I often start with a knitting technique book or books and pictures with decorations. From that point, I begin sketching. I don't have a particular system in which fashion, decoration or knitting technique comes first. Often the result is something totally different than what I had in mind when I began the sketches.

– We have design programs in our contemporary world of computers, some of which are completely ideal for me. It helps me to 'see' the final result before I begin to knit. If I have the time and opportunity, I try to knit the garment myself and often discover new and hopefully better ideas while the work is in progress. In most cases, we don't have time for me to knit everything, but I always knit a swatch which gives a good idea of what the finished result will be. I do the finishing and other details myself so I can focus on each aspect on even a simple design.

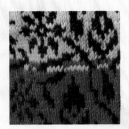

ARAN SWEATER

The sweater's hip sections are knitted separately, so that there are slits in the sides. Then the body is knitted in the round up to the armholes, after which the back and front are worked separately back and forth. The sleeves also have slits at the lower edges, but the rest is knitted in the round. The edges around the slits are crocheted and can be fastened with buttons.

SIZES
S (M) L

Total circumference: 44 (46 1/2) 49 1/2in
112 (118) 126cm

Total length: 27 1/4 (28) 28 3/4in
69 (71) 73cm

Sleeve length: 18 1/2 (19) 19 1/4in
47 (48) 49cm

MATERIALS
Vamse yarn (100% pure new wool – 83 metres per 50 g) from Rauma Ullvarefabrikk:

brown (64) 950 (1000) 1050 g

Needles: circular ndls 7 and 9 (4.5 and 5.5mm), a cable neeedle, plus crochet hook F (4mm).

Notions/haberdashery: 10 buttons

Gauge/tension: 24 sts = 4 x 4in/10 x 10cm in pattern on ndls 5.5mm

Be sure that your gauge is correct! Change to larger or smaller needles if necessary.

PATTERN
Chart A shows the pattern for the hip sections. Chart B shows the body front and back and C shows the yoke front. Charts D and E show the entire sleeve. On the charts, sizes are marked by arrows and dark lines. Follow the arrows and marking lines for your size.

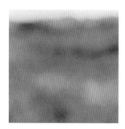

Hip Sections
With circular ndl 7 (4.5mm), CO 130 (138) 146 sts. Working back and forth, knit 2 rows (= 1 ridge). Continue, following the pattern on chart A: Begin at the right side for all sizes and knit to the arrow for your size on the left side, ending with P1 on sizes S + M. Finish the pattern when the work measures about 5in/13cm (last row = wrong side). Then knit 2 rows and, at the same time, CO 2 new sts at each side = 134 (142) 150 sts. Set the piece aside and work another to match.

Body: With ndl 9 (5.5mm), work in the round over all 268 (284) 300 sts. Place a marker at the beginning of the rnd. Continue, following chart B over the sts for the front: Size S – begin with P3, work the pattern between the arrows and finish with P3. Size M – begin with P4, K1tbl, P2, work the pattern between the arrows and finish with P2, K1tbl, P4. Size L – Work the sts between the arrows. Place a marker after these sts and work the sts for the back. When the piece measures 16 (17) 17 3/4in/41 (43) 45cm from the cast-on row, divide the piece at the side markers for the armholes and then work back and forth on each side separately.

Front: Continue working back and forth in pattern B until the work measures about 23 1/4 (24) 25in/59 (61) 63cm from the cast-on (last row = wrong side). Change to ndls 7 (4.5mm) and knit 2 rows; on the 2nd row dec to 132 (140) 148 sts with the decs evenly spaced across.

Then knit the yoke following chart C: begin at the right side for all sizes and knit to the arrow on the left side, finish the P2 on sizes S + M.

When the yoke measures 3/4in/2cm, BO the centre 28 sts for the neck. **NOTE:** On the chart, the neck is correctly positioned for size L. Work each side separately, back and forth and, at the beginning of each row at the neck edge, BO 4-2-2-1-1-1 sts. Finish the pattern when the yoke measures about 3 3/4in/9.5cm (the last row = wrong side). Knit 2 rows and then BO for the shoulders.

Back: Worked as for the front, except that the yoke measures about 3in/7.5cm when you bind off for the neck. BO the centre 44 sts and work each side separately. On every row at the neck edge, BO 2-1 sts. Finish when the back is the same length as the front.

Sleeves
With ndls 7 (4.5mm), CO 50 sts. Working back and forth, knit 2 rows (= 1 ridge). Continue working back and forth following chart D. Finish the pattern when the work measures about 3 1/4in/8cm (last row = wrong side).
Then knit 2 rows and CO 2 new sts on each side + inc 2 (4) 6 sts evenly spaced on the last row = 56 (58) 60 sts. Change to ndls 9 (5.5mm) and continue working in the round, following chart E and knitting the sts between the arrows for your size. Inc 2 sts at the underarm every 4th rnd for the entire length. These sts are knitted when there are not enough sts for a cable. BO when the sleeve measures about 18 1/2 (19) 19 1/4in/47 (48) 49cm.

Finishing
Carefully steam all the pieces on the wrong side between damp towels. Sew the shoulders together.

Collar: With ndls 7 (4.5mm), CO 30 sts. Work back and forth in K2, P2 ribbing until the piece measures 26 3/4in/68cm. BO in ribbing. Sew the collar to the neck opening with the ends overlapping, so that they are doubled over the 28 bound-off sts at the centre front. Sew the collar securely and turn the collar outwards (see photo). Split edges: Single crochet along the open side of the hips – 3 rows along the back and 5 rows along the front but, on the 3rd row along the front, make 3 buttonholes with chain sts. Crochet corresponding edges along the slits on the sleeves, but with 2 buttonholes. Sew on the buttons and sew in the sleeves.

ARAN SWEATER

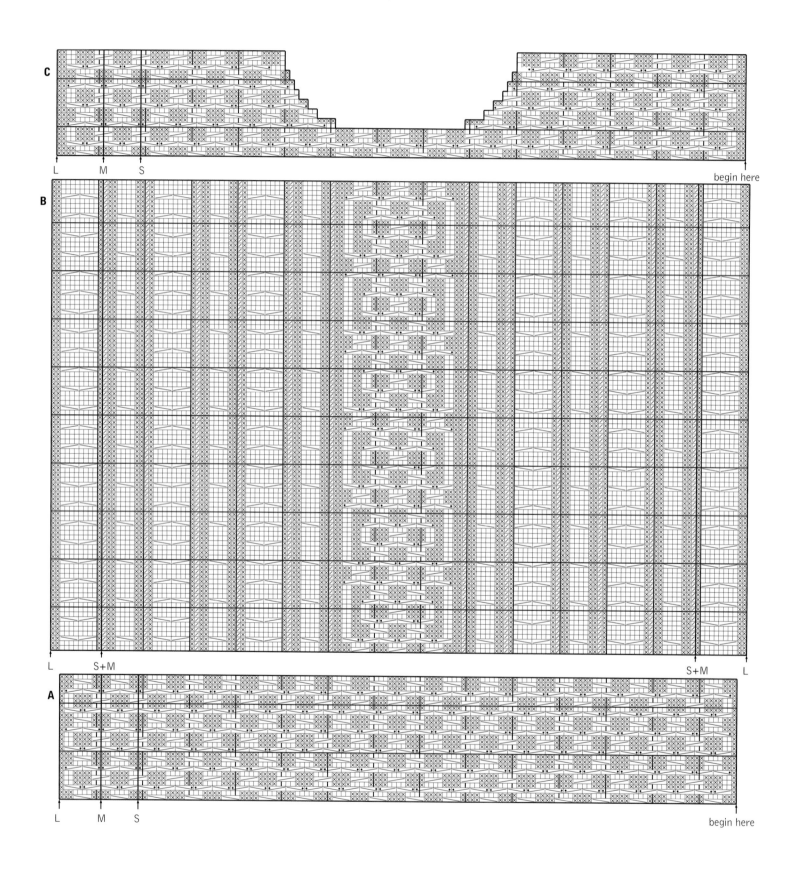

ARAN SWEATER

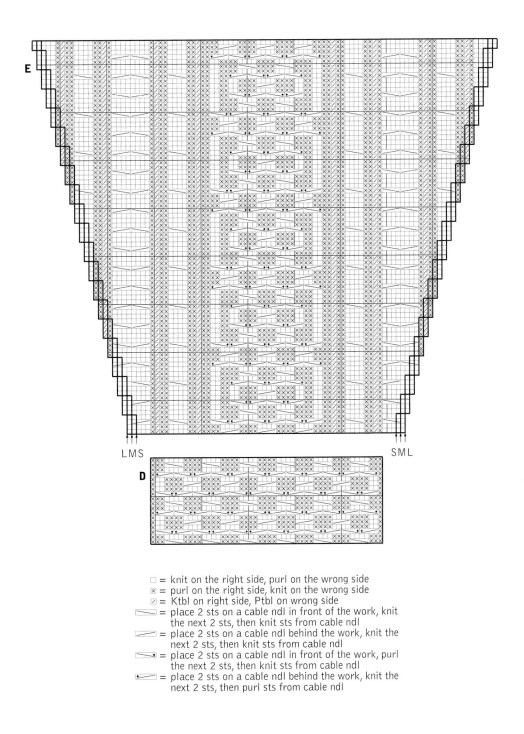

E

LMS   SML

D

☐ = knit on the right side, purl on the wrong side
⊠ = purl on the right side, knit on the wrong side
☑ = Ktbl on right side, Ptbl on wrong side
⬭ = place 2 sts on a cable ndl in front of the work, knit
     the next 2 sts, then knit sts from cable ndl
⬭ = place 2 sts on a cable ndl behind the work, knit the
     next 2 sts, then knit sts from cable ndl
⬭ = place 2 sts on a cable ndl in front of the work, purl
     the next 2 sts, then knit sts from cable ndl
⬭ = place 2 sts on a cable ndl behind the work, knit the
     next 2 sts, then purl sts from cable ndl

The jacket body is knitted in the round up to the armholes and then worked back and forth. The sleeves are knitted in the round. The cuffs and peplum sections – 2 on each front and 3 on the back – are knitted last.

SIZES
S/M (M/L)

Total circumference:	39 1/2 (42 1/2)in	100 (108)cm
Length from shoulder to waist:	15 3/4 (16 1/2)in	40 (42)cm
Underarm length:	17 3/4 (18 1/2)in	45 (47)cm

MATERIALS
Rauma 3-ply Strikkegarn (100% pure new wool – 108 metres per 50 g) from Rauma Ullvarefabrikk:

black (136)	450 (500) g
red (174)	50 (50) g
lacquer red (124)	50 (50) g
orange (161)	50 (50) g
yellow (131)	50 (50) g
yellow-green (198)	50 (50) g
green (130)	50 (50) g
turquoise (183)	50 (50) g
blue (167)	50 (50) g
blue-violet (142)	200 (200) g
red-violet (141)	50 (50) g

Needles: circular and dpn 2 (3mm) and 4 (3.5mm).
Notions/haberdashery: 7 clasps to fasten the front opening.
Gauge/tension: 24 sts and 26 rows = 4 x 4in/10 x 10cm in stockinette and pattern on ndls 4 (3.5mm).
Be sure that your gauge is correct! Change to larger or smaller needles if necessary.

PATTERN
Chart A shows the body front and back; chart B shows the pattern for the sleeves, cuffs and peplum pieces. Sizes on the body are marked with arrows and dark lines. Follow the arrows and marking lines for your size.

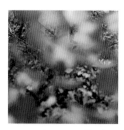

Body
With black and ndls 2 (3mm), CO 195 (215) sts. The first and last 2 sts on the rnd (4 sts) are the centre front steek and are always knitted with black without any patterning up to the neckline. Work in the round in stockinette following chart A: Begin after the 2 steek sts at the centre st of the pattern, knit to the arrow for your size on the left side (= right front) and place a marker; beginning at the arrow on the right side after the marker, knit to the arrow on the left side (= back) and place a marker; beginning again at the arrow on the right side after the marker, knit to and including the centre st (= left front) + 2 steek sts. **NOTE:** The rows marked with the minus (–) sign are not knitted on size S/M. After the 3rd (5th) rnd, change to ndls 4 (3.5mm). Inc 1 st on each side of the markers every 4th rnd 10 times as shown on the chart (= 4 sts increased per rnd) – inc by picking up the thread between sts and placing it on the left ndl; knit through back loop. At the arrow marking the armhole, BO 8 sts on each side (= 4 sts on each side of the markers) and finish the rnd. Cut yarn and continue, working back and forth, doing the front and back separately.

Fronts: Begin at the underarm and work back and forth. Dec for the armhole at the beginning of each row at each side: BO 2 sts once and 1 st 4 (6) times. At the arrow marking the neckline, BO the centre 32 sts (including the steek sts) and work each side separately. At the beginning of each row at the neck edge, BO 3-2-2-1-1-1-1 sts. Work to the end of the chart and BO the remaining 23 (26) sts for the shoulders with black.

Back: Bo for the underarm in the same way as for the front. At the arrow marking the neckline, BO the centre 43 sts and work each side separately. At the beginning of each row, at the neck edge, BO 1-1-1 st. Work to the end of the chart and BO the remaining sts with black.

Sleeves
With black and ndls 4 (3.5mm), CO 49 (53) sts. Knit the stripe pattern for the entire sleeve following chart B. Inc 2 sts centred at the underarm every 4th rnd for the entire length. Work the increased sts into the striped pattern as set. When the sleeve measures 17 3/4 (18 1/2)in/45 (47)cm, divide the piece at the centre of the underarm and work back and forth. BO for the sleeve cap at the beginning of each row on each side 3-2-1-1-1-1 sts. BO the remaining sts knitwise.

Cuffs: Turn the sleeve inside out and pick up and knit 51 (55) sts from the wrong side with black and ndls 4 (3.5mm). Working back and forth, purl 3 rows (the 2nd row will be purled on the right side for the turning row). Continue in stockinette in stripe pattern B and, at the same time, inc 1 st on each side of the cuff every 4th row 6 times. Work the increased sts into the striped pattern as set. When the cuff measures about 3in/7.5cm from the turning row and the last row is on the wrong side, continue in stockinette: 2 rows black, 1 row yellow-green and 2 rows black. Continue with black – knit 1 row on the wrong side for the turning row and then work 6 rows in stockinette for the facing. BO. Lightly steam the sleeves and cuffs on the wrong side. With black and ndls 2 (3mm), pick up and knit 20 sts along each of the cuff's short sides. In stockinette, work 1 row black, 1 row yellow-green and 2 rows black. Continue with black and knit 1 row on the wrong side for the turning row and then work 6 rows in stockinette for the facing. BO. Lightly steam on the wrong side. Turn the cuffs to face the right side and sew then along the turning row, so that they are held in place and so that the short sides overlap at the turning edges.

Finishing
Machine-stitch two lines on each side of the centre of the front steek and cut between the lines.
Peplum sections: With black, ndls 2 (3mm), and right side facing beginning 1 st before the steek sts on the left front, pick up and knit 21 (23) sts in the cast-on row. Knit stripe pattern B in stockinette, working back and forth – 23 (25) rows. Continue in stockinette – 2 rows black, 1 row yellow-green, and 2 rows black. Continue with black and purl 1 row on the right side for the turning row and then work 6 rows in stockinette for the facing. BO. Pick up and knit 23 (25) sts along the side edge of the peplum section, from the body down to the turning row. In stockinette, work 1 row black, 1 row yellow-green and 2 rows black. Continue with black and knit 1 row on the wrong side for the turning row and then work 6 rows in stockinette for the facing. BO. Make another section of the peplum: skip 4 sts on the cast-on row of the body and, with black and ndls 2 (3mm), pick up and knit 21 (23) sts. The section ends 2 (3) sts from the side marker. Work as for the previous peplum section but work the edging on both sides of the piece. Knit corresponding peplum sections on the right front. The peplum sections on the back are worked similarly, with each ending 2 (1) sts from the side marker and the middle one worked over the centre 41 (49) sts of the back (skip 4 sts from the sections at the sides) and worked in the same way as the other sections.
Front bands: With black and ndls 2 (3mm), pick up and knit 95 (99) sts along the front edge, from the turning row on the peplum and up to the neckline. In stockinette, work 1 row black, 1 row yellow-green, and 2 rows black. Continue with black and knit 1 row on the wrong side for the turning row and then work 6 rows in stockinette for the facing. BO. Knit a matching band on the other front. Turn the facings to the inside and sew them neatly on the wrong side.
Neckband: With black and ndls 2 (3mm), pick up and knit 31 sts along the neckline on the right front, 52 sts on the back and 31 sts along the neck line of the left front. In stockinette, work 5 rows black, 1 row yellow-green, and 2 rows black. Continue with black and knit 1 row on the wrong side for the turning row and then work 9 rows in stockinette for the facing. BO. Turn the facing to the inside and sew it carefully on the wrong side. Sew in the sleeves. Sew 7 clasps on the inside of the front bands with the lowest one at the waistline.

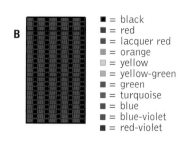

B

■ = black
■ = red
■ = lacquer red
■ = orange
□ = yellow
■ = yellow-green
■ = green
■ = turquoise
■ = blue
■ = blue-violet
■ = red-violet

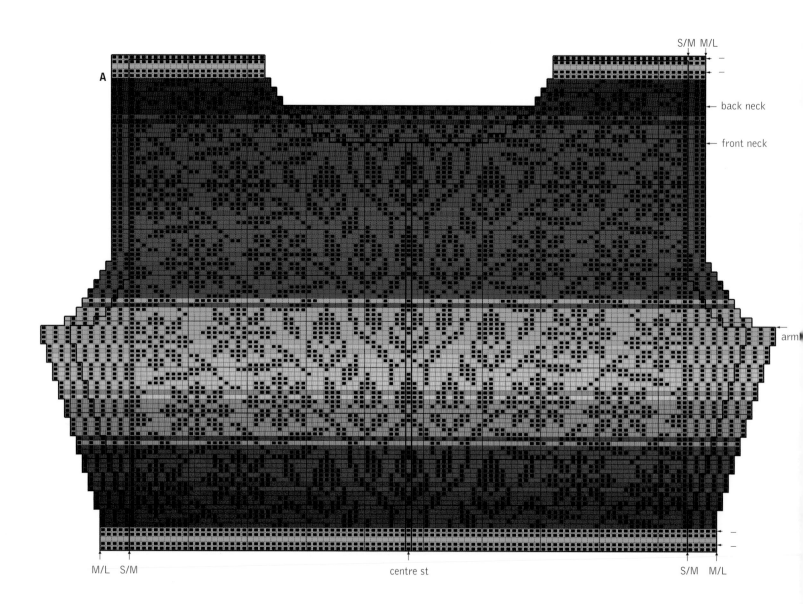

S/M M/L

A

back neck

front neck

arm

M/L S/M

centre st

S/M M/L

DESIGNER'S BACKGROUND AND INSPIRATION

Iselin Hafseld
Born in 1960.

Education
Graduated from the Oslo National Academy of the Arts in 1986, specializing in clothing design.

Publications
Norsk Strikkedesign (1999) and *Strikk fra TINDE* (2017)

Professional Work
Iselin Hafseld is the founder of the brand TINDE, which was launched in 1996. TINDE is known for high quality knitwear collections, available in Scandinavia and parts of Europe.
In 1988, Iselin established the design label NORI, together with Kirsti Bræin. The design-duo collaborated up to 1995, and participated in a number of shows, exhibitions and competitions with great success.
Besides developing her own knitwear collections for TINDE and NORI, Iselin has designed for knitwear manufacturers, yarn companies and magazines.
She has been Examiner at the Oslo National Academy of the Arts and also member of the jury for design competitions.

Awards
1985: First prize in 'Certina Creative Challenge', arranged by the fashion magazine TIQUE and CERTINA.
1988: Second prize prize in the Jubilee competition for Dale of Norway.
1990–1993: NORI has, for four consecutive years, won the first prize in the competition for the official World Cup and Olympic sweaters for the ski team, produced by Dale of Norway.
1991: Norwegian Form's Annual Prize for Creativity and New Thinking to the design-duo NORI.
1992: First prize for the official Ski team World Cup sweater 1993, produced by Dale of Norway.
1996–1998: First prize, three years running, for designing the Skating team's World Cup sweater, produced by IDENA AS Knappehuset.

Shows and Exhibitions
Iselin has participated in several exhibitions and shows in Norway and abroad, including: 'Fashion, Trends and Designers', exhibition at the Art-Industry Museum and City-Hall in Oslo, 2000; 'Glowing Colours and Glistening Gold', Art-Industry Museum in Oslo 1998; participated with knitwear at 'Kjell Torheim's Jubilee Show', Oslo, 1996; Norwegian Days in Lund and Malmö, Sweden 1996; 'Breaks', Art-Industry Museum, Trondheim 1995; 'Troll Straw and Old Women Spinning', Maihaugen, Lillehammer 1993–94; NORI-show at the IGEDO fair, Düsseldorf, 1993; 'Moments of Norwegian Pattern', Prague 1992; 'Knitting the Norwegian Way', Stockholm, 1992; 'Passion on Circular Needles', travelling exhibit in Norway, 1991–92; 'KK's Jubilee Show', Oslo, 1990; 'Crossing Point', Høvikodden 1991; 'Clothing and Jewelry', Oslo, 1989.

Iselin's designs have been purchased by the National Institute of Fashion Technology, New Delhi, India.

On Designing
– The inspiration for the blue sweater in blue tones (see pages 66–69) was Harald Solberg's 'Winter Night in Rondane'. The ornamentation is a combination of rosemaling motifs found on old Norwegina chests and Arabic designs. On the finished garment, simple stars were embroidered in the night sky with contrasting colours.

– The inspiration for the black and white sweater (see pages 70–73) was taken from the many rose-patterned sweaters found in Norway. The pattern here was made larger than those usually seen on the sweaters. The main background colour should be light and the pattern defined with darker shades. In addition, I wanted to add additional colour in the sweater; some are introduced in the knitted borders, others are embroidered. The embroidery was done last on the completed garment.

SHORT SWEATER IN BLUE TONES

The sweater is knitted in the round up to the neckline and then cut open for the armholes. It can be knitted in two colours for the main pattern and the details in other colours embroidered on later with duplicate stitch. The model has special rolled bands at the lower edges of the body and sleeves and around the neck.

SIZES

S (M)

Total circumference:	56 1/4 (56 1/4)in	143 (143)cm
Total length:	20 1/2 (21 1/4)in	52 (54)cm
Sleeve length:	17 1/2 (17 3/4)in	44 (45)cm

MATERIALS

Rauma 3-ply Strikkegarn (100% pure new wool – 108 metres per 50 g) from Rauma Ullvarefabrikk:

marine blue (159)	350 (400) g
turquoise (182)	300 (300) g
violet (142)	50 (50) g
dark green (185)	50 (50) g

+ small amount of olive (7/61).

Needles: circular and dpn 1 (2.5mm) and 5 (4mm), plus a small circular ndl 2 (3mm).

Gauge/tension: 22 sts and 25 rows = 4 x 4in/10 x 10cm in stockinette and pattern on ndls 5 (4mm).

Be sure that your gauge is correct! Change to larger or smaller needles if necessary.

PATTERN

Chart A shows the body front and back; chart B shows the entire sleeve; chart C is the pattern repeat for the neckband. Sizes are marked on the pattern with arrows and dark lines. Follow the arrows and marking lines for your size.

Body

With violet and ndls 1 (2.5mm), CO 202 (210) sts; join. Working stockinette in the round, knit 8 (12) rnds. These rows are formed into a doubled edge as follows: using an extra needle, pick up 1 st from the cast-on row and knit it with 1 st from the main needle; continue in this way around. Change to dark green yarn and knit 6 (8) rnds. Make a rolled edging by picking up sts from the first dark green rnd with an extra needle and knitting it with a dark green st from the main ndl. **NOTE:** It is important to pick up the same number of sts on the auxiliary needle as there are on the body and to be sure that the sts which are knitted together are directly parallel, so that the edging doesn't bias. Change to ndl 5 (4mm) and knit 1 rnd with marine blue and, at the same time, inc 20 (32) sts evenly spaced around = 222 (242) sts. Place a marker at each side, so that there are 111 (121) sts each for the front and back. Continue knitting, following chart A: beginning at the arrows on the right side (both at the side and under the chart), knit to the arrow on the left side (= front); inc 1 st with turquoise (side st). Begin at the arrows on the right side again and knit the sts for the back; inc 1 st with turquoise (= side st). The side sts are knitted with turquoise for the entire length. Inc 1 st on each side of the side sts (= 4 inc per rnd). For size S, inc every other rnd 16 times and then every 3rd rnd 8 times; for size M: inc every 3rd rnd 19 times.

At the arrow for the neckline, BO the centre 17 sts on the front, then finish the rnd and begin the next row at the neck. Work back and forth and, at the beginning of every row at the neck edge, BO 3-3-2-2-1-1-1 sts. There is no back neckline. After completing the charted rows, BO knitwise with marine blue.

Sleeves

With violet and ndls 1 (2.5mm), CO 45 (49) sts; join. Knit a doubled edging with violet and a rolled edge with dark green as for the body. Change to ndls 5 (4mm) and knit the pattern following chart B between the arrows marking your size, but CO 1 extra st with turquoise at the centre of the underarm. This st is knitted with turquoise for the entire length of the sleeve and is not included in the charted pattern. Inc 1 st on each side of the centre st at the underarm every 3rd rnd 24 times and then every other rnd 16 times. After completing the charted rows, continue with marine blue – knit 1 rnd and then purl 4 rnds for the facing. BO.

Finishing

Lightly steam the pieces on the wrong side. Embroider the colour details in duplicate st following the charts for both the body and sleeves. Without stretching them, mark the width at the top of the sleeves on each side of the body from the shoulders downwards and baste a line for the armhole. Machine-stitch two lines on each side of the basting thread and cut the sleeve opening between them. Sew the shoulders together and sew in the sleeves. Sew the facings loosely over the cut edges on the wrong side. Lightly steam the seams.

Neckband: With marine blue and ndls 2 (3mm) pick up and knit 104 (108) sts around the neck opening. Knit border pattern C, making certain that the centre st on the pattern comes at the centre front; repeat *–* around. **NOTE:** At the same time, dec 2 sts at each shoulder on every other rnd a total of 2 times = 96 (100) sts. When the border pattern has been completed, knit a rolled edge with dark green as follows: Knit 4 rnds stockinette, pick up sts from the 2nd rnd (knitted with dark green) and, using violet, knit 1 st from each needle together. Then knit another 4 rnds with violet and make a new rolled edge by picking up sts from the 1st rnd with violet. Knit 1 st from each needle together with violet. Change to marine blue and knit 6 rnds stockinette for the facing – inc 2 sts at each shoulder every other rnd a total of 2 times. When the facing is long enough, BO loosely. Turn the facing to the inside and sew it loosely on the wrong side.

Lightly steam the neck.

SHORT SWEATER IN BLUE TONES

■ = marine blue
■ = turquoise
■ = olive (can be knitted on the neckband)
⊠ = knit with marine blue, embroider with olive
⊠ = knit with marine blue, embroider with violet
■ = knit with marine blue, embroider with dark green
⊠ = knit with turquoise, embroider with violet
⊠ = knit with turquoise, embroider with olive

centre st

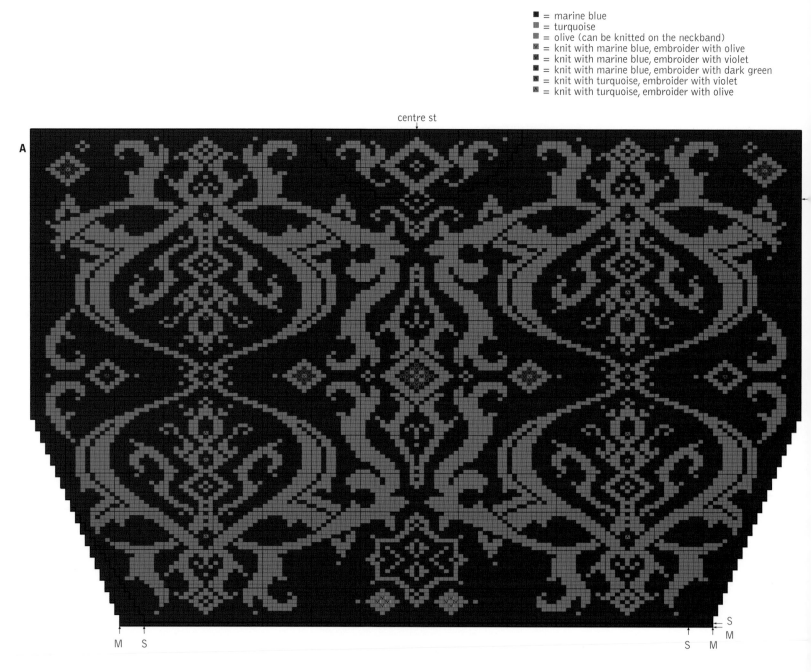

A

M S

S M

SHORT SWEATER IN BLUE TONES

SHORT, WIDE SWEATER WITH COLLAR

The sweater is knitted in the round up to the neckline and then the front and back are worked back and forth separately. It is cut open for the armholes afterwards. The main pattern can be knitted in two colours. The other colours are embroidered on in duplicate stitch after the knitting has been completed.

SIZES
S (M) L

Total circumference:	46 (49) 52in	117 (124) 132cm
Total length:	22 1/2 (23 5/8) 24 3/4in	57 (60) 63cm
Sleeve length:	19 3/4 (20) 20in	50 (51) 51cm

MATERIALS
Peer Gynt (100% pure new wool – 91 metres per 50 g) from SandnesGarn:

natural white (664)	600 (650) 700 g
black (18)	300 (350) 400 g
olive (295)	50 (50) 50 g
yellow-beige (218)	50 (50) 50 g
rust (337)	50 (50) 50 g
light blue (905)	50 (50) 50 g

Needles: circular and dpn 1 (2.5mm) and 5 (4mm), small circular ndl 2 (3mm) plus a crochet hook C (3mm).
Notions/haberdashery: a clasp about 2 1/2in/6cm wide.
Gauge/tension: 22 sts and 24/25 rows = 4 x 4in/10 x 10cm in stockinette and pattern on ndls 5 (4mm).
Be sure that your gauge is correct! Change to larger or smaller needles if necessary.

PATTERN
Chart A shows the front and back of the body; chart B shows the entire sleeve; border C, which is at the top of the sleeve, is also used for the neckband. The sizes are marked on the charts with arrows and dark lines. Follow the arrows and marking lines for your size.

Ribbed Border: (no of sts divisible by 4)
Row 1: *K3, P1; repeat from * around.
Row 2: P1, *K1, P3; repeat from * around, ending with P2.
Repeat these 2 rows for the pattern.

Body
With natural white and ndls 1 (2.5mm), CO 216 (228) 240 sts; join. Work 3 1/8in/8cm in the ribbed border described above. Change to ndls 5 (4mm) and inc 22 (26) 30 sts evenly spaced around = 238 (254) 270 sts. Place a marker at each side so that there are 119 (127) 135 sts each for the front and back. Knit the pattern following chart A: Beginning at the arrow for your size at the right side, knit to the arrow on the left side (= front). Beginning again at the arrow on the right side after the marker, knit the sts for the back. Inc on each side of the markers as shown on the chart (= 4 sts increased per rnd). At the arrow for the neckline, divide the work at the side markers and knit the front and back separately, back and forth.
Back: Work, following the chart, until 6 rows before the arrow for the shoulders. BO the centre 23 (25) 27 sts for the neck and work each side separately. At the beginning of each row at the neck edge, BO 5 sts 2 times = 43 (46) 49 sts for each shoulder. Finish at the arrow for your size; work 1 row natural white and BO.

Front: Continue following the chart, but BO the centre 17 (19) 21 sts and work each side separately. At the beginning of each row at the neck edge, BO 3 sts 3 times, then 2 sts twice = 43 (46) 49 sts for each shoulder. Finish at the arrow for your size; work 1 row natural white and BO.

Sleeves
With natural white and dpn 1 (2.5mm), CO 52 (56) 60 sts; join. Work 2 3/4in/7cm of the ribbed border as for the body. Change to ndls 5 (4mm) and inc 3 sts evenly spaced around = 55 (59) 63 sts. Continue, knitting the pattern on chart B between the arrows for your size. Inc 2 sts centred at the underarm as the chart shows until there are 113 (117) 121 sts. **NOTE:** On size S, do not knit the last 3 rows before border pattern C. When border C has been completed, continue with natural white. Knit 1 rnd and then purl 4 rnds for the facing. BO.

Finishing
Lightly steam the pieces on the wrong side. Embroider the extra colour areas in duplicate st following the charts for both the body and sleeves. Without stretching them, mark the width at the top of the sleeves on each side of the body from the shoulders downwards and baste a line for the armhole. Machine-stitch two lines on each side of the basting thread and cut the sleeve opening in between them. Sew the shoulders together and sew in the sleeves. Sew the facings loosely over the cut edges on the wrong side. Lightly steam the seams.
Collar: with natural white and ndl 2 (3mm), pick up and knit 121 sts around the neck opening, beginning at the centre of the front. The collar is worked back and forth with the opening centred at the front. Knit 1 row with natural white and then work the border pattern C following the chart. **NOTE:** BO 2 sts at each shoulder every 3rd row a total of 3 times = 109 sts remaining. When the border pattern has been completed, inc 2 sts at the centre back = 111 sts. Continue with natural white and work about 3 1/2in/9cm of the ribbed border as for the body, but working back and forth instead. BO.

Finally, with natural white, crochet 2 rows of sc around the split collar opening. Sew a clasp at the border pattern at the lower edge of the collar.

SHORT, WIDE SWEATER WITH COLLAR

□ = natural white
■ = black
■ = olive
▩ = yellow-beige
■ = knit with background colour, embroider with rust
■ = knit with background colour, embroider with light blue
■ = knit with background colour, embroider with olive
▨ = knit with background colour, embroider with yellow-beige

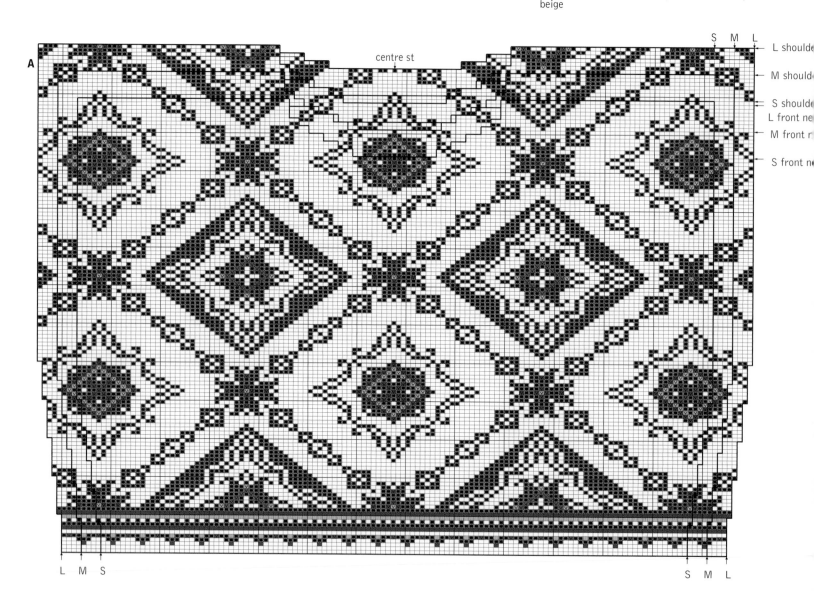

centre st

A

S M L

L shoulder

M shoulder

S shoulder
L front neck

M front neck

S front neck

L M S

S M L

SHORT, WIDE SWEATER WITH COLLAR

ISELIN HAFSELD

DESIGNER'S BACKGROUND AND INSPIRATION

Irene Haugland Zahl
Born in Telemark in 1954.

Education
After studying at the National Handicraft and Art-Industry School in Oslo, Irene trained to be a fashion designer and specialized in knitting design. Her Telemark background was an early inspiration for incorporating Norwegian folk art elements and folklore into her designs.

Publications
Strikk fra Telemark (2015), published in the USA as *Knits From The Heart Of Norway* (2015, Trafalgar Square Books).

Professional Work
For many years, she has been one of the leading designers for Dale of Norway. Her designs include official sweaters for the Olympics and the World Cup.

In 1993, Irene and her husband established the firm, Vrikke, in Eydehavn. The company produces collections of her own designs, including knitted sweaters, jackets, skirts and mittens, many of which feature embroidered rose patterns.

The past twenty-two years she has designed clothing (both knitwear and embroidered) in China and Litauen.

On Designing
– The design for the jacket 'Eydehavn' (see pages 76–79) was inspired by a folk costume. I own dozens of folk costume books, all of which are frequently used for inspiration and are endless sources for ideas.

First and foremost, the jacket was inspired by my own east-Telemark costume. The colours – red, black and mustard yellow – predominate. The jacket is also short, just a traditional folk costume's would.

The lovely, sterling clasps echo the costume's silver brooches.

– Folk costume is also the inspiration for 'Lunde' (see pages 80–83), which is a sweater with a pleated welt and decorative bands. Certainly, for a while now, Sami costumes have been a strong source of inspiration. This sweart has a 'skirt' often see in Lappland costume and a markedly short, boxy body.

Initially, I designed several Sami-inspired models. This is the latest one and is a continuation of the previous designs.

The idea behind the design is also to add non-traditional elements to the knitted models.

'EYDEHAVN' PATTERNED JACKET

The jacket is knitted in the round to the neckline and then cut open for the armholes and centre front. The pattern can be knitted in two colours. The other colours are embroidered with duplicate and chain stitches afterwards. The model has doubled picot edgings which form a border for the lower bands, on the shoulders and around the front opening.

SIZE
M

Total circumference:	45 1/4in	115cm
Total length:	22in	56cm
Sleeve length:	17 1/4in	44cm

MATERIALS
Vestlandsgarn (100% pure new wool – 100 metres per 50 g) from Gjestal Spinneri

red (209)	400 g
olive (245)	350 g
grey (205)	100 g
natural white (200)	50 g
black (201)	300 g
green (213)	50 g
orange (239)	50 g

Needles: circular and dpn 1 (2.5mm), 2 (3mm), and 4 or 5 (3.5 or 4mm).
Notions/haberdashery: 3 clasps – 2 3/8in/6cm wide.
Gauge/tension: 23 sts and 27 rows = 4 x 4in/10 x 10cm in stockinette and pattern on ndls 4 or 5 (3.5 or 4mm).
Be sure that your gauge is correct!

PATTERN
Charts A + B show the right front and half of the back. Charts C + D show the entire sleeve. The first repeat shows how the pattern is knitted; the rest of the chart shows how the bands will be embroidered as part of the finishing.

Body
With black and ndl 1 (2.5mm), CO 261 sts; join. The 3 centre sts at the beginning of the row are the steek and are worked throughout with no patterning and in one colour. Work 27 rnds in stockinette for the facing, and an eyelet row for the turning: *K2tog, yo; repeat from * around, not including the 3 steek sts (begin and end the rnd with K2tog on each side of the steek sts). Then work 4 rnds in stockinette with black. Change to ndl 2 (3mm) and knit pattern border A – repeating from *–* around. On the last rnd, inc to 267 sts (total includes the steek sts) with the incs evenly spaced around.
Change to black and knit a doubled picot edge as follows: Knit 4 rnds in stockinette; an eyelet row as for the turning at the lower edge; then 4 rnds stockinette. The edge can be doubled on the last rnd by using an extra ndl to pick up sts from the first rnd in black, on the wrong side. With black, knit 1 st from the main ndl with one st from the extra ndl around the whole row (= 4 rnds after the eyelet row). Or you can sew the first and last rnds together on the wrong side when finishing the jacket.
Change to ndl 4 or 5 (3.5 or 4mm) and continue the pattern following chart B: beginning at the right side of the chart after the steek, knit to the centre st, then work back from the centre st (= centre back).
At the arrow marking the armhole, BO 1 st each side. CO 4 new sts over the bound-off ones for the armhole steek and continue around. The steek is knitted without any patterning for the entire length. At the arrow marking the neckline, BO the centre 53 sts on the front (including the steek sts). Begin working back and forth. At the arrow marking the back neck, BO the centre 43 sts on the back and then work each side separately.

On the last row of the chart, BO the armhole steek sts + 1 st on each side of the neck opening on both the front and back. Place the shoulder sts for the back on a holder. On each front shoulder, knit a doubled edging with an eyelet row with black and ndl 1 (2.5mm), in the same way as for the lower edge of the body but work 3 rows after the eyelet row and place the sts on a holder for later finishing.

Sleeves
With black and dpn 1 (2.5mm), CO 74 sts; join. The first st on the rnd is the centre underarm st. Knit 27 rnds in stockinette for the facing, decreasing 2 sts centred at the underarm (with the centre st in between the incs), every 3rd rnd 9 times = 56 sts. Then knit an eyelet row for the turning: *K2 tog, yo; repeat from * around. On the next 23 rnds, inc 2 sts (1 inc at each side of the centre underarm st), alternately every 2nd and 3rd rnds until there are 74 sts. Begin with 4 rnds black (the first inc is on the 2nd rnd). Change to ndls 2 (3mm) and work border pattern C in grey and white as for the body. When border C is complete, you should have 74 sts on the ndl. Change to black and knit a doubled picot edge as on the body.
Change to ndls 4 or 5 (3.5 or 4mm) and continue, following chart D. Inc 2 sts at the underarm (with 1 st in between), alternately every 3rd and 4th rnds until there are 128 sts. After completing the charted rows, use red to knit 1 rnd and purl 4 rnds for the facing. BO loosely.

Finishing
Machine-stitch two lines on each side of the centre front and armhole steeks. Cut up between the lines. Lightly steam the pieces on the wrong side before you embroider the details. Embroider using chain and duplicate sts as indicated on the charts for the body and sleeves – see detail photo.
Turn the facings on the lower edges of the body and sleeves to the inside and sew them neatly on the wrong side. With black, weave the sts of the shoulders together (= last row with black for the doubled picot edges). Arrange the doubled edge so that the first and last rows will be sewn together with black on the wrong side.
Bands: With black and ndls 1 (2.5mm), pick up and knit about 120 sts on the right side of each front edge. Working back and forth, work 4 rows stockinette, an eyelet row for the turning and 6 rows stockinette for the facing. BO. Turn the facings to the inside and sew them loosely over the raw edges on the wrong side.
Neckband: With black and ndl 1 (2.5mm), pick up and knit 158 sts around the neck opening (also picking up sts over the front bands) – 28 sts along each front, 26 sts along each shoulder, 46 sts on the back neck + 1 st at each corner. Work 4 rows stockinette back and forth, and at the same time, dec 1 st at each side of each corner on every row – dec by K2tog tbl before the corner st, knit the corner st, then K2tog. Next, work an eyelet row for the turning and 5 rows stockinette for the facing – inc to mirror-image the decs at each corner. BO loosely. Turn the facing to the inside and sew it neatly on the wrong side. Sew in the sleeves and sew the facing over the raw edges on the wrong side. Sew the clasps on. Spread the garment to finished measurements between damp towels and lay flat to dry.

'EYDEHAVN' PATTERNED JACKET

IRENE HAUGLAND ZAHL

IRENE HAUGLAND ZAHL

'EYDEHAVN' PATTERNED JACKET

■ = grey
□ = natural white
■ = red
■ = olive

▨ = duplicate st embroidery with olive
▨ = duplicate st embroidery with green
▨ = duplicate st embroidery with orange

■ = chain st embroidery with red
■ = chain st embroidery with black
◉ = chain st embroidery with orange

centre st

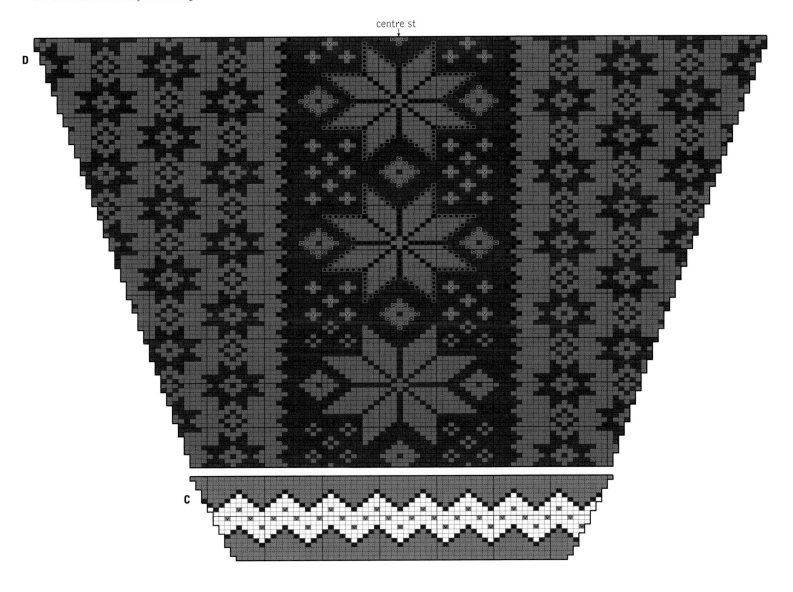

IRENE HAUGLAND ZAHL

'LUNDE' SWEATER WITH PLEATED WELT AND DECORATIVE BANDS

The sweater is knitted in the round to the neckline, and then cut open for the V-neck and armholes. The pleated welt and decorative band on the lower part of the body are knitted separately and then sewn on. Embellishments on the sleeves and welt are embroidered in chain stitch before the sweater is assembled.

SIZE
M

Total circumference:	45 1/4in	115cm
Total length:	29 1/2in	74cm
Sleeve length:	19 1/4in	49cm

MATERIALS
Vestlandsgarn (100% pure new wool – 100 metres per 50 g) from Gjestal Spinneri:

grey (205)	600 g
natural white (200)	450 g
black (201)	450 g
red (209)	150 g
olive (245)	50 g
green (213)	50 g
orange (239)	50 g

Needles: circular and dpn 1 (2.5mm) and 4 or 5 (3.5 or 4mm).
Gauge/tension: 23 sts and 27 rows = 4 x 4in/10 x 10cm on ndls 4 or 5 (3.5 or 4mm) in stockinette and pattern.
Be sure that your gauge is correct!

PATTERN
Chart A shows the pleated welt; B the decorative bands; and C the entire front; D + E show the entire sleeve. Border pattern B is also knitted on the neckband.

Pleated Welt
With black and ndl 1 (2.5mm), CO 576 sts; join. Knit 9 rnds for the facing and purl 1 rnd for the turning row. Change to ndls 4 or 5 (3.5 or 4mm). Work pattern A, repeating the section *–* around. The first repeat shows how the pattern is knitted in grey and white, then it shows how each repeat will be embroidered with the other colours afterwards. When the pattern rows have been completed, knit 3 rnds with grey. BO loosely.

Decorative band: with black and ndl 1 (2.5mm), CO 264 sts; join. Knit 30 rnds for the facing. Change to ndl 4 or 5 (3.5 or 4mm) and purl 1 rnd for the turning. Knit border pattern B: Beginning at the right side of the chart, repeat from *–* around. Continue with black and purl 1 rnd for the turning. Change to ndl 1 (2.5mm) and knit 12 rnds for the facing. BO loosely.

Body
With grey and ndls 4 or 5 (3.5 or 4mm), CO 264 sts; join. Working in the round, knit 3 rnds with grey before you begin the pattern. Place a marker at each side, with 133 sts for the front and 131 sts for the back. Work pattern C following the chart: Beginning at the right side, knit to the left side (= front); repeat the section between the asterisks (*–*) across the sts on the back.
At the arrow for the neckline, BO the centre st on the front. On the next rnd, CO 3 new sts over the bound-off st for the V-neck's steek and continue working in the round. The steek sts are always knitted in one colour without any patterning. V-neck: on every other rnd, dec 1 st at each side of the 3 steek sts 35 times – dec with K2tog tbl before the steek and K2tog after the steek. At the arrow marking the armhole, CO 4 new sts at each side for the armhole steek. Continue knitting in the round in pattern, but do not work any patterning on the steek sts.
At the arrow for the neckline, BO the steek sts at the centre front and the 63 centre sts on the back for the neck and then work each side separately, back and forth. Dec 1 st at the beginning of each row at the neck edge, 3 times. BO all remaining sts for the shoulders when the pattern rows have been completed.

Sleeves
With black and dpn 1 (2.5mm), CO 80 sts; join. Knit 44 rnds for the facing, decreasing 2 sts at the underarm (with 1 st in between the decs) on every 4th rnd, 8 times and then every 3rd rnd, 4 times = 56 sts. Change to ndls 4 or 5 (3.5 or 4mm) and purl one rnd for the turning. Continue with the centre st at the underarm in the background colour in pattern for the whole length (this st is not shown on the chart). Knit pattern D. Inc 2 sts centred at the underarm (with 1 st in between) every 3rd rnd, 10 times and then every 4th rnd for the rest of the length. When pattern D has been completed, purl 1 rnd with black. Continue with pattern E following the chart. The pattern can be knitted in grey and white (as for the welt). The chart shows how the diamond motifs will be embroidered afterwards. If you want to shorten the sleeves, begin pattern E further up from the lower edge so that you will have a complete diamond at the top of the sleeve. After completing the charted rows, continue with grey and knit 1 rnd and then purl 4 rnds for the facing. BO loosely.

Finishing
Carefully steam all the pieces on the wrong side. Embroider the centres of the diamond patterns on the sleeves and welt with chain st as shown on the detail photo.
Machine-stitch on each side of the V-neck and armhole steeks and cut up the centre of each steek. Sew the shoulders together with backstitch from the wrong side. Turn in the facings at the lower edges of the welt and sleeves and carefully sew to the wrong side.
Neckband: with black and ndl 4 or 5 (3.5 or 4mm), CO 221 sts; join. Knit 1 rnd and purl 1 rnd (= 1 ridge). Then knit pattern border B following the chart – begin at the arrow marking the neck edge and repeat from *–* around, except for the last 4 sts which are worked without patterning for the steek. When the pattern rows are complete, continue with black and purl one rnd for the turning. Change to ndls 1 (2.5mm) and knit about 5 1/2in/14cm for the facing. BO loosely. Machine-stitch on each side of the steek and cut up the centre of the steek. Turn the raw edge to the inside.
With black, sew the band carefully around the neck from the right side as follows: begin at the centre of the V-neck, sew up along the left side of the neck, around the back neck, and down the right side. At the centre front, sew the band down at the inside of the black border pattern (see photo). Turn the facing to the wrong side and sew it down loosely.
Sew the sleeves in with backstitch from the wrong side and then sew the facing smoothly over the cut edges on the wrong side.
Pleated welt and decorative band: Pleat the welt so that all the embroidered patterns meet centred over the stripe/block sections. Baste the pleats around the top of the welt and steam carefully. Sew the facings together at the back of the red decorative band and steam it lightly.
Baste and then sew the welt to the decorative band and then attach the band to the body with small sts and black yarn. Be sure that the centre st on each of these pieces matches the centre st on the front of the body.

GENSER MED KAPPE OG DEKORKANT LUNDE

'LUNDE' SWEATER WITH PLEATED WELT AND DECORATIVE BANDS

C

← back neck

← armhole

← front neck

centre front

B

centre front

neck edge

A

centre front

82

GENSER MED KAPPE OG DEKORKANT LUNDE

IRENE HAUGLAND ZAHL

'LUNDE' SWEATER WITH PLEATED WELT AND DECORATIVE BANDS

■ = black
■ = grey
□ = natural white
■ = red
■ = green
■ = orange
■ = olive

■ = chain st embroidery with red
▣ = chain st embroidery with green
▣ = chain st embroidery with orange
▣ = chain st embroidery with olive

centre st

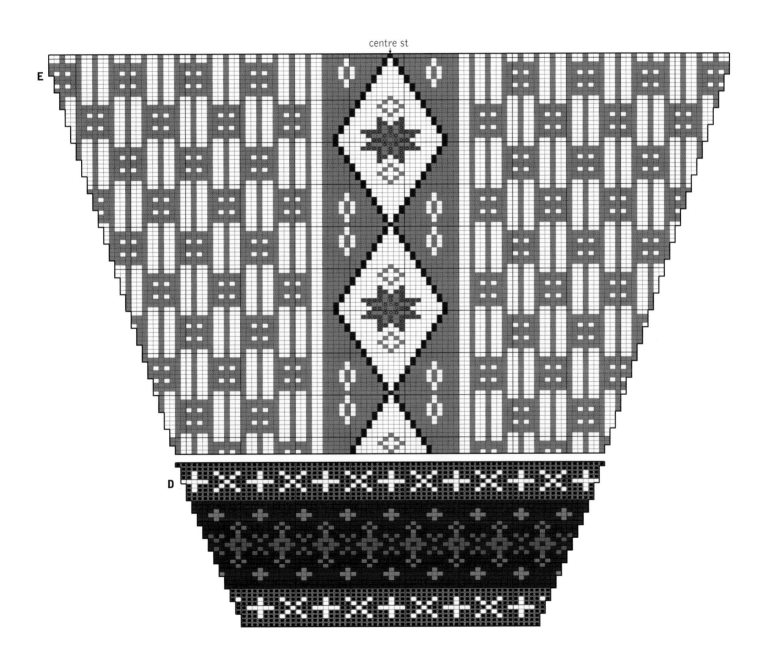

DESIGNER'S BACKGROUND AND INSPIRATION

Anne Helene Gjelstad
Born in Oslo in 1956.

Education
Trained in sewing and weaving at the National Handicraft and Art-Industry School, Institute for Clothing and Costume.

Scholarships
Artist Stipend in 1985, 1987, 1990, 1994 and 1997.
Norwegian Cultural Council's Equipment Stipend in 1988 and 1992.
Technical Literature Society's Travel Scholarship in 1999.

Publications
Everything about Machine Knitting (1994).

Professional Work
Anne Helene has done costume design, sewing and scenography for TV, film, and theater. She has also had a close working relationship with the fashion designer William and participated in several fashion shows and art-handicraft exhibitions.

In 1988, together with Eva Lie, Anne Helene established the company Our Atelier. She has had several commissions for the Norwegian textile industry as well as projects involving design, sewing and knitting for artists and private customers, including Queen Sonja.

Anne Helene has designed knitted pieces for most of the Norwegian yarn companies. She has produced sewing and knitting projects and done styling and illustration for magazines and worked as a technical journalist.

She has her own handknitted collection, Borealis of Norway.

On Designing
– I am most often inspired by folkloric traditions from the entire world. The traditional and the unique, which are a part of our old cultural heritage, piques my curiosity and brings out the joy of creating. It is fantastic to see how different cultures use the same patterns, but how each creates a special expression with it. The starting point for a design is something which captures my interest. It can be an old garment, a beautiful fabric, a colourway or, quite simply, a mood or feeling. An art exhibit, a few hours at a museum, a conference visit, a round of the boutiques or a tour out in nature always give me inspiration. I take a great deal of pleasure from the old knitting books and handwork pamphlets I've collected.

– 'From Selbu to the Sahara'
The idea for this sweater (see pages 86–89) was the desire to combine a folkloric pattern from different cultures into a common expression. The bird and flower patterns come from old women's costumes which were worn by Bedouins in North-Africa. I've re-worked the patterns and set them together with other elements, including the eight-petalled rose – the world's most-used pattern which, for us Norwegians, goes under the name 'Selbu rose'.

– 'Carpathian Black Roses'
The main pattern in this model (see pages 90–93) comes from traditional embroideries of Transylvania, recorded before the First World War but certainly even older. I've reworked the pattern, added and removed elements, and also experimented a lot with colours before I ended up with this result. The styling was also important. The jacket should be wearable by most people and I wanted to join the folkloric with the modern. Therefore, the model has a feminine element, a zippered front opening, and collar and cuffs with looped crochet.

Photo from book *Palestinian Costume* by Jehan Rajab

Photo from book *Palestinian Costume* by Jehan Rajab

85

ANNE HELENE GJELSTAD

FROM SELBU TO THE SAHARA

The sweater, with bird designs from the Sahara and the eight-petalled rose from Selbu, is knitted in the round to the neck and then cut open for the armholes. The square neckline is finished with a doubled stockinette band. The ribbed bands at the bottom of the body and sleeves have a simple cable pattern.

SIZES
S/M (L/XL)

Total circumference:	48 1/2 (52)in	123 (132)cm
Total length:	24 (24 1/2)in	61 (62)cm
Sleeve length:	19 1/4 (19 1/2)in	49 (50)cm

MATERIALS
Telemark (100% pure new wool – 140 metres per 50 g) from SandnesGarn:
black (612)   450 (500) g
beige (623)   350 (400) g
Needles: circular and dpn 1 (2.5mm).
Gauge/tension: 27 sts and 31 rows = 4 x 4in/10 x 10cm in stockinette and pattern on ndls 1 (2.5mm).
Be sure that your gauge is correct! Change to larger or smaller needles if necessary.

PATTERN
Chart A shows the body front and back, B shows the entire sleeve. The sizes are marked on the charts with arrows and dark lines. Follow the arrows and marking lines for your size.

Ribbed border with cables: multiple of 6 sts.
Row 1: P1, *K4, P2; repeat from * around, ending with P1.
Row 2: as row 1.
Row 3: P1, *place 2 sts on a cable ndl in front of the work, knit the next 2 sts and then knit the 2 sts from the cable ndl, P2; repeat from * around, ending with P1.
Row 4: as row 1.
Repeat from the first row until you have turned the cables 5 times; end with row 4.

Body
With black and circular ndl 1 (2.5mm), CO 294 (318) sts; join. Work the ribbed band with cables as explained above. Then place a marker at each side with 147 (159) sts between them. Knit 2 sts on each side of the markers with black without any patterning for the entire length. Work pattern following chart A: knit 1 side st; begin at the arrows for your size at the right side (arrows at the side and beneath the chart); work the front to the arrows on the left side; K2 side sts; begin at the arrows on the right side again and knit across sts for the back, ending with a side st. Inc 1 st at each side of the side sts, every 8th rnd, 10 times = 334 (358) sts.
At the arrow for the front neck, BO the centre 37 sts on the front and finish the rnd. Cut yarn. Begin the next row at the neck opening and continue, working back and forth.
At the arrow for the back neck, BO the centre 37 sts on the back and work each side separately. BO with black after completing the charted rows.

Sleeves
With black and dpn 1 (2.5mm), CO 78 (78) sts; join. Work the ribbed band with cables as for the body. Inc 5 (9) sts evenly spaced around the last rnd = 83 (87) sts. Knit the 2 sts at the underarm in black for the entire length of the sleeve. Work pattern following chart B: begin at the arrows for your size at the right side ((arrows at the side and beneath the chart). Inc 1 st at each side of the 2 underarm sts every 4th rnd until there are 149 (155) sts on the ndl. After completing the charted rows, continue with black only and purl 6 rnds for the facing. BO.

Finishing
Spread the pieces to finished measurements between damp towels. Lay flat until dry. Mark the length for the armholes and baste from the shoulders down to the marker. Machine-stitch two lines on each side of the basting thread and cut between them. Sew the shoulders together. Sew the sleeves in with mattress stitch on the right side; turn the facings over the raw edges on the wrong side and sew them down loosely.
Neckband: starting at the shoulder seam, right side facing, with black and ndl 1 (2.5mm), pick up and knit 34 sts on each side of the neck and 1 st in each of the bound-off front and back neck sts = 142 sts; join. Knit 4 rnds, decreasing 8 sts on the 2nd and 4th rnds by working K2tog tbl before each corner and K2tog after each corner. Purl 1 rnd for the turning and then knit 5 rnds for the facing – inc 2 sts at each corner on the 2nd and 4th rnds. BO. Turn the facing to the inside and sew it loosely on the wrong side.
Lightly steam all the seams under a damp cloth on the wrong side.

A

S/M

L/XL

S/M
L/XL

L/XL S/M

S/M L/XL

FROM SELBU TO THE SAHARA

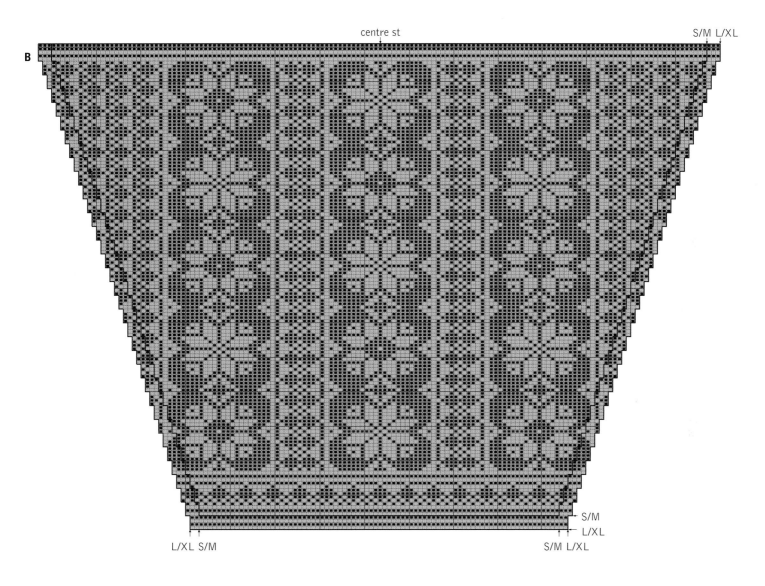

= black
= beige
= black on the front, beige on the back

CARPATHIAN BLACK ROSES

The jacket is knitted in the round to the underarms and then the front and back are worked back and forth. The centre front is cut open afterwards. The pattern is knitted in red and black and the other colours are later embroidered with duplicate stitch. The collar and cuffs are knitted in garter stitch and then chain stitch crocheted frills are worked into the garter stitch ridges.

SIZES

S (M) L

Total circumference:	39 3/4 (42) 44 1/2in	101 (107) 113cm
Hip circumference:	41 (43 3/8) 44 1/2in	104 (110) 113cm
Total Length:	23 5/8 (24 1/4) 25 1/4in	60 (62) 64cm
Underarm length:	19 (19) 19 1/2in	48 (48) 49cm

MATERIALS

Hifa 2 (100% pure new wool – 315 metres per 100 g) from Hillesvåg Ullvarefabrikk:

red (6013)	300 (350) 400 g
black (6053)	300 (300) 350 g
green (6089)	50 (50) 50 g
blue (6082)	50 (50) 50 g
ochre (6093)	50 (50) 50 g

Needles: circular and dpn 0 and 1 (2 and 2.5mm) and crochet hook B (2.5mm).
Notions/haberdashery: a 19 3/4 (19 3/4) 21 1/2in/50 (50) 55cm strong, black, zipper.
Gauge/tension: 26 sts and 35 rows in lice pattern and 32 rows in the main pattern = 4 x 4in/10 x 10cm on ndls 1 (2.5mm).
Be sure that your gauge is correct! Change to larger or smaller needles if necessary.

PATTERN

Chart A shows the body front and back; chart B shows the entire sleeve. The sizes are marked on the charts with arrows and dark lines. Follow the arrows and marking lines for your size.

Body

With black and circular ndl 0 (2mm), CO 270 (286) 302 sts; join. Knit 7 rnds for the facing; purl 1 rnd for the turning. Place a marker at the beginning of the rnd (= centre front), one after 68 (72) 76 sts and another after 135 (143) 151 sts (= side markers). Move the markers up as you work. Change to ndl 1 (2.5mm) and continue in stockinette. Knit the first 5 rnds on chart A: beginning at the centre front, knit to the arrow for your size on the left side (= right front); beginning after the marker at the arrow on the right side, knit to the arrow on the left side (= back); begin at the arrow on the right side again after the marker and finish the rnd (= left front). There are no extra sts for the steek at the centre front.
After completing the border, follow the arrow at the right side of the chart which shows on which row of the lice pattern to start for your size. Adjust the pattern so it looks the nicest – with either complete or no lice at each side. Dec at the sides as shown on the chart – K2tog tbl before the side marker and K2 tog after the side marker (= 4 decs each time). After the decs, there are 242 (258) 274 sts on the ndl. Continue, increasing on each side of the side markers as indicated on the chart. After the increases, there should be 262 (278) 294 sts on the ndl. At the arrow for the armhole, BO as follows: Knit 59 (63) 67 sts, BO 14 sts, knit 117 (125) 133 sts; BO 14 sts and finish the rnd. Cut yarn.
Work the back and front separately, back and forth. Begin the row at the armhole.

Front: At the beginning of each row at each armhole edge, dec 4-2-1-1-1-1 sts. Inc for the shoulders as shown on the chart.
At the arrow for the neckline, BO the centre 11 (13) 15 sts and work each side separately. Continue decreasing at the beginning of each row at the neck edge 4-2-2-1-1-1-1-1 sts. Shape the shoulders as shown by decreasing at the beginning of each row at the shoulder edge.
Back: Worked as for the front except for the neckline. Bind off for the back neck on the row indicated by the arrow. First BO the centre 23 (25) 27 sts and then work each side separately. Continue, decreasing at the beginning of each row at the neck edge 4-2-1 sts.

Sleeves

With ndl 1 (2.5mm) and black, CO 53 (55) 59 sts. Working back and forth, knit 35 rows garter st (= 18 ridges). Inc 6 sts evenly spaced on the last row = 59 (61) 65 sts. Join and continue working in the round. Following chart B, knit the sts between the arrows for your size. Inc at the underarm as the chart shows until there are 105 (107) 111 sts on the ndl. Work to the arrows for your size, then BO the centre 8 (6) 6 sts at the underarm. Work the sleeve cap back and forth, decreasing as shown on the chart.
Frilled cuffs: Join the ridged edges at the lower edges of the sleeves. Hold the piece upside down and begin crocheting in the 2nd ridge from the patterned knitting: Crochet *1 slip st, ch 5, skip 1 st; repeat from * around. Crochet loops in the same way on every other ridge, using slip sts to move between the ridges.

Collar

With black and ndl 1 (2.5mm), CO 119 (123) 127 sts. Working back and forth, work 3 rows in stockinette for the facing. Place a marker at the centre back

and continue in garter st (knit every row). When the piece measures 3/4in/2cm, inc 1 st in the 2nd and 2nd to last sts (= edge sts), and 1 st on each side of the centre back st (= 4 incs per row). Repeat the incs at each side every 3/8in/1cm and at the centre back every 3/4in/2cm. Knit a total of 21 ridges (including the binding off) and BO.
Frilled edging: Beginning on the right side of the ridge nearest the facing, crochet loops as for the sleeves, but cut the yarn at the end of each row and crochet all the frills starting at the right side so that the loops will all turn the same way.

Finishing

Spread the pieces to finished measurements and gauge between damp towels. Lay flat to dry. Embroider the details in green, blue and and ochre with duplicate st following the charts.
Machine-stitch 2 lines on each side of the centre front of the body and cut between the lines. Turn the lower facing on the body to the inside and sew it loosely on the wrong side. Sew the shoulder seams with back stitch on the wrong side.
Bands: Right side facing, with black and ndl 0 (2mm), pick up and knit about 134 (140) 146 sts along the front. CO an extra st at the lower edge for the seamline. Work 3 rows in stockinette, purl 1 row on the right side for the turning and 3 rows stockinette for the facing. BO. Turn the facing to the inside and sew it loosely over the raw edges on the wrong side. With black sewing thread, sew the zipper in by hand firmly but carefully so that the sts do not show on the right side.
Sew in the sleeves.
Lay the collar with its wrong side facing the right side of the garment. Using backstitch and black yarn, sew the collar along the first row of loops – begin at the centre back and sew one side, then sew the other side. Sew the facing down on the wrong side. Lightly steam block the jacket under a damp cloth.

A

back neck

front neck

S M L

S armhole
M armhole
L armhole

S

M

L

BORDER

L M S

centre st

S M L

ANNE HELENE GJELSTAD

CARPATHIAN BLACK ROSES

■ = red
■ = black
■ = knit with red, embroider with green
■ = knit with red, embroider with blue
■ = knit with red, embroider with ochre

DESIGNER'S BACKGROUND AND INSPIRATION

Kari Haugen
Born in Telemark in 1952.

Education
Kari was trained at the Bergen Art-Handicraft School.

Professional Work
She is a designer for Dale of Norway, having first worked there freelance and then in a permanent position.

Exhibitions
She has participated in several exhibitions, including 'Passion on Circular Needles', 1991–92.

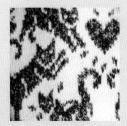

CHILD'S SWEATER WITH A CAT PATTERN

The sweater is knitted in the round to the neckline and cut open for the armholes afterwards. The pattern is different on the front and back. The red edgings are crocheted on as part of the finishing.

SIZES

4 (6) 8 years

Total circumference:	30 (33) 35 1/2 in	
	76 (84) 90cm	
Total length:	15 3/4 (17 3/4) 19 1/4in	
	40 (45) 49cm	
Sleeve length:	12 1/4 (13 3/8) 14 1/2in	
	31 (34) 37cm	

MATERIALS

Vestlands yarn (100% pure new wool – 100 metres per 50 g) from Gjestal Spinneri:

natural white (200)	250 (300) 350 g
salt & pepper (227) or tweed (299)	150 (200) 250 g
red (240)	50 (50) 50 g

Needles: circular and dpn 1 (2.5mm) and 2 or 4 (3 or 3.5mm); crochet hook A (2mm).
Gauge/tension: 24 sts and 28 rows = 4 x 4in/10 x 10cm in stockinette and pattern.
Be sure that your gauge is correct!

PATTERN

Chart A shows the front of the body; chart B shows the back and C shows the left sleeve.
The sizes are marked on the charts with arrows and dark lines.
Follow the arrows and marking lines for your size.

Body

With natural white and ndl 1 (2.5mm), CO 184 (200) 216 sts; join.
Work 1 1/2in/4cm in ribbing: K1tbl, P1.
Change to ndl 2 or 4 (3 or 3.5mm) and continue in stockinette. Knit 1 rnd in natural white and then work the pattern following charts A and B: Beginning at the arrows (at both the side and beneath the chart) for your size at the right side of chart A, knit to the arrows on the left side (= front) and place a marker; after the marker, begin at the arrows for your size at the right side of chart B and finish the rnd (= back).
At the arrow for the front neck, BO the centre 16 (18) 18 sts at the centre front and finish the rnd. Cut yarn and then work back and forth. Begin the row at the neck opening. Continue decreasing at the neck edge at each side as shown on the chart. At the arrow for the back neck, BO the centre 30 (34) 34 sts of the back and then work each side separately. On the next row, BO 1 st at the neck edge.
Finish the pattern at the arrow for your size and place the shoulder sts on a holder.

Sleeves

Left sleeve: with natural white and dpn 1 or 2 (2.5 or 3mm), CO 46 (46) 48 sts; join. Work 1 1/2in/4cm in ribbing: K1tbl, P1. Change to dpn 2 or 4 (3 or 3.5mm) and continue in stockinette. Knit 1 rnd natural white and then follow chart C between the arrows for your size. Inc 2 sts at the underarm every 4th rnd, 18 (20) 15 times and then every 3rd rnd 10 times on size 8 yrs.
Finish the pattern at the arrow for your size or to desired sleeve length.
Continue with natural white – 2 rnds stockinette and 3 rnds purl for the facing.
Right sleeve: CO and knit as for the left sleeve, but reverse the pattern on the chart, so that for both sleeves the light background colour is on the front and the dark background on the back.

Finishing

Steam the pieces on the wrong side. Mark the length for each armhole and baste from the shoulder down to the marker. Machine-stitch 2 lines on each side of the basting thread and cut between the lines. Weave the shoulder sts together. Sew in the sleeves and sew the facings loosely over the raw edges on the wrong side.
Neckband: with natural white and ndl 1 (2.5mm), pick up and knit 86 (90) 90 sts around the neck opening; join. Work ribbing (K1tbl, P1) for 1 1/8in/3cm. Work an eyelet row for the turning: *K2tog tbl, yo; repeat from * around. Work another 1 1/8in/3cm in twisted ribbing for the facing and BO loosely. Turn the facing along the eyelet row and sew the facing loosely on the wrong side.
Crocheted edgings: The edges are finished in red yarn and crochet. Crochet around the neck opening in this manner: *insert the crochet hook into a purl st in the 3rd row of sts from the top edge; 1 sc, ch 1, skip over 1 knit st; repeat from * around. Be sure that the sts are not too tight or causing the ribbing to draw in!
Lower edges of body and sleeves: *insert the crochet hook into the 4th purl st from the bottom, sc 1, ch 4, skip 1 knit st + 1 purl + 1 knit; repeat from * around.

BARNEGENSER I KATTEMØNSTER

CHILD'S SWEATER WITH A CAT PATTERN

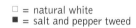

□ = natural white
■ = salt and pepper tweed

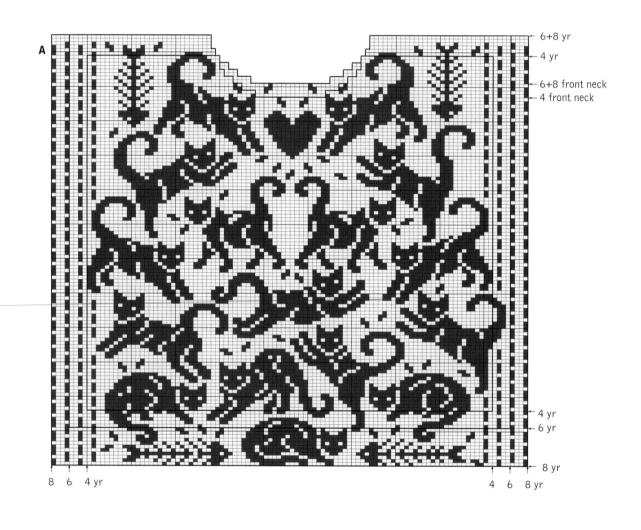

KARI HAUGEN

CHILD'S SWEATER WITH A CAT PATTERN

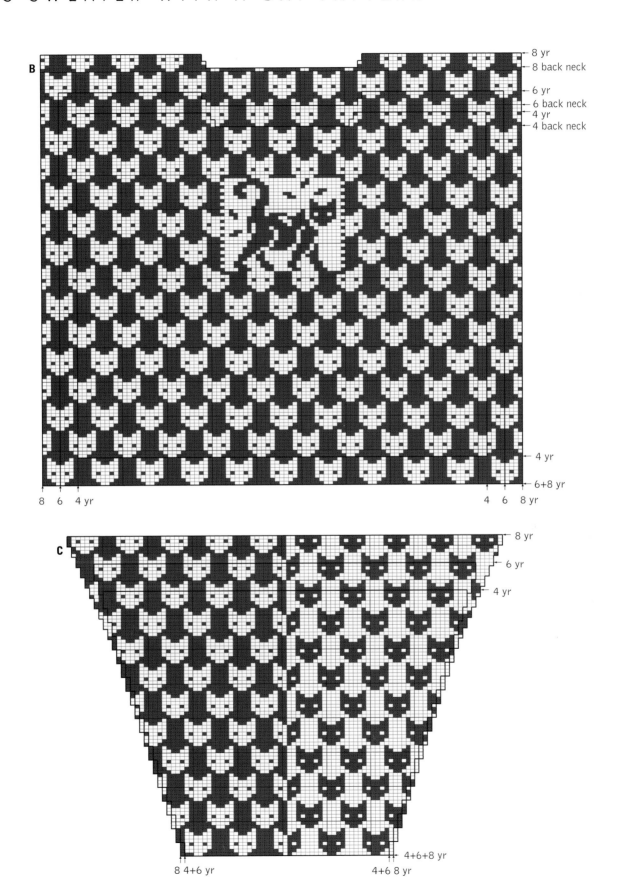

KARI HAUGEN

FITTED EMBROIDERED JACKET

The jacket is knitted in the round upwards from the scalloped lower edge and then cut open at the centre front and armholes. The design can be knitted in two colours and the details in the other colours embroidered with duplicate stitch. The scroll lines are embroidered with chain stitch.

The jacket in the photo is size M. For sizes S and L, the main pattern is unsymmetrical, but it is only conspicious before you work the embroidery. On these sizes, you only need to embroider the borders, yoke and sleeves.

SIZES
S (M) L

Total circumference: 37 3/4 (39 3/4) 42 1/8in
          96 (101) 107cm
Total length: 25 1/2 (26 3/8) 27 1/4in
          65 (67) 69cm
Underarm length: 15 3/4 (16 1/2) 17 1/4in
          40 (42) 44cm

MATERIALS
Istra Kamgarn (100% pure new wool – 105 metres per 50 g) from Rauma Ullvarefabrikk:

dark green (2085)	400 (450) 500 g
cinnamon brown (2098)	250 (300) 350 g
yellow (2048)	100 (100) 100 g
green (2032)	100 (100) 100 g
turquoise (2052)	50 (50) 50 g
red (2074)	50 (50) 50 g
light beige (2008)	50 (50) 50 g
grey-brown (2009)	50 (50) 50 g

Needles: circular and dpn 1 (2.5mm) and 2 or 4 (3 or 3.5mm).
Notions/haberdashery: 7 (7) 8 tin buttons.
Gauge/tension: 24 sts and 28 rows = 4 x 4in/10 x 10cm in stockinette and pattern.
Be sure that your gauge is correct!

PATTERN
The scalloped edge is knitted and then the band and rest of the body are knitted following the charts. Charts A and B show the patterns for the body, C + D + E show the yoke and F shows the entire sleeve. Sizes are marked on the charts for the yoke and sleeves with arrows and dark lines. Follow the arrows and marking lines for your size.

Body
With green and circular ndl 2 or 4 (3 or 3.5mm), CO 273 (289) 305 sts. Work back and forth and work 9 rows of the scalloped edge as follows:
Row 1 (wrong side): K across. **Row 2:** K1 *yo, K6, K3tog, K6, yo, K1; repeat from * across. **Row 3:** P across. **Row 4:** same as row 2. **Row 5:** change to turquoise and knit one row on the wrong side. **Row 6:** same as row 2. **Row 7:** P across. **Row 8:** same as row 2. **Row 9:** K on the wrong side.
CO 4 new sts at the centre front for the steek; join and work stockinette in the round. The steek sts are worked without patterning for the entire length. Knit border pattern A: begin after the steek on the right side of the chart and repeat from *–* around, but dec 1 st at the centre of the first rnd = a total of 8 1/2 (9) 9 1/2 repeats of 32 sts each.
Place a marker after every 16th st around = 16 (17) 18 markers. Continue, following chart B: begin after the steek with the centre front band, then work across as shown on the chart, repeating from *–* until there are 16 pattern sts remaining; finish the rnd with a reverse of the centre front band = a total of 7 1/2 (8) 8 1/2 repeats between the front bands. On rnd 2, dec 1 st on each side of the markers – K2tog tbl before the marker and K2tog

after the marker = 32 (34) 36 sts decreased on each rnd. Continue, following the chart and decreasing as above, just as the chart shows – **NOTE:** there is no decreasing before the first or after the last marker = 30 (32) 34 sts decreased per row. Work the increases as shown on each repeat = 225 (238) 251 sts when chart B has been completed.

Yoke: The yoke consists of 3 sections, which are worked at the same time as follows: Begin at the centre front band on pattern C and knit to the arrow for your size (= right front), continue with pattern D between the arrows (= back), and then work across pattern E from the arrow, to and including the front band (= left front). After 1 (2) 3 rnds, BO for the underarm: Knit 51 (54) 57 sts, BO 10 (9) 10 sts, knit 103 (111) 117 sts, BO 10 (10) 10 sts, knit 51 (54) 57 sts + 4 steek sts.
On the next rnd, CO 4 new sts over the bound-off sts at each underarm for the armhole steeks. Continue working in the round. Work the armhole decs at each side of the steeks: On the fronts, dec 1 st every rnd 4 (2) 2 times, then every other rnd 3 (4) 2 times and on every 4th rnd 0 (0) 1 time. At the same time, dec on the back –1 st at each side every rnd 3 (3) 3 times, then on every other rnd 4 (4) 2 times and on every 4th rnd 0 (0) 1 time = 44 (48) 52 sts for each front and 89 (97) 105 sts on the back.
At the arrow for the neckline, BO the centre 28 (34) 40 sts on the front (including the steek sts) and begin working back and forth. Work the neck decs at the beginning of each row at each side – 2 sts 2 (2) 1 times and 1 st 3 (2) 3 times. At the arrow for the shoulder row, BO the armhole steek and then work each side separately. Shape the shoulders by BO at the shoulder, every row 5-5-5-5-5 (5-5-5-6-6) 5-6-6-6-6 on each shoulder. At the same time, at the arrow for the back neck, BO the centre 33 (37) 41 sts and work each side separately. Continue with the neck decs on every other row, 2-1 sts.

Sleeves
With green and dpn 1 (2.5mm), CO 60 (64) 68 sts; join. Work 6 rnds of K1, P1 ribbing. Change to dpn 2 or 4 (3 or 3.5mm) and work the pattern following chart F – between the arrows for your size. After completing the yellow border, inc 3 sts at the underarm. Then inc 2 sts at the underarm (with 2 sts between the increases) every 7th rnd until there are 85 (91) 97 sts on the ndl. Work to the arrow for your size and BO 10 (10) 12 sts centred at the underarm. CO 4 new sts over the bound-off sts for the sleeve cap steek and continue working in the round. Dec for the sleeve cap on each side of the steek sts as follows: Size S: 1 st on every rnd 3 times, knit 2 rnds, dec 1 st on the next rnd, (K 3 rnds, dec 1 st on the next rnd) 6 times, (K 1 rnd, dec 1 st on the next rnd) 2 times, then dec 1 st on each on the next 2 rnds. BO the steek sts and work back and forth. Continue decs at the beginning of every row on each side 2-2-3-5 sts. BO the remaining 23 sts knitwise on the right side. Size M: dec 1 st on every rnd 4 times, K 1 rnd, dec 1 st on the next rnd, (K 3 rnds, dec 1 st on the next rnd) 6 times, (K 1 rnd, dec 1 st on each rnd) 5 times. BO the steek sts and work back and forth. Continue decreasing at the beginning of every row at each side 2-2-3-5 sts. BO the remaining 25 sts knitwise on the right side. Size L: dec 1 st on every rnd 4 times (K 1 rnd, dec 1 st on the next rnd) 2 times, (K 3 rnds, dec 1 st on the next rnd) 4 times, (K 1 rnd, dec 1 st on the next rnd) 4 times, dec 1 st on every rnd 4 times. BO the steek sts and work back and forth. Continue decs at the beginning of every row at each side 2-2-3-5 sts. BO the remaining sts knitwise on the right side.

Finishing
Steam the pieces on the wrong side. Machine-stitch 2 lines on each side of the centre front steek on the body, on the armholes, and sleeve caps; cut between the lines. Embroider the pieces before you assemble the jacket.

FITTED EMBROIDERED JACKET

Fill in 'flowers' and 'leaves' with duplicate st as shown on the chart, using red, green and yellow yarn. For the scroll lines around the 'acanthus vines', split the yarn into 2 strands and stitch small chain sts with grey-brown, light beige and green yarn – see detail photo. Weave the shoulders together. Sew the sleeves neatly into the body, preferably by machine. Cover the raw edges of the sleeve cap with buttonhole st or sew a cotton band over the raw edges on the wrong side.

Front bands: with dark green, ndl 1 (2.5mm), and right side facing, pick up and knit about 24 sts per 4in/10cm along the right front. Knit 1 row on the wrong side; work 3 rows stockinette; knit 1 row on wrong side for the turning and then 4 rows stockinette for the facing. BO and sew the facing neatly on the

wrong side. Work the band for the left front in the same way.

Neckband: with dark green, ndl 1 (2.5mm), and right side facing, pick up and knit about 123 (129) 135 sts. Work 7 rows of K1, P1 ribbing and then an eyelet row for the turning: *K2tog, yo; repeat from * across, ending with K1. Work another 8 rows of ribbing for the facing. BO in ribbing. Turn the facing along the eyelet row and sew it neatly on the wrong side. Make 7 (7) 8 button loops on the right front band, with the top one centred on the neckband and the others with 2 3/4–3in/7–8cm in between each. Sew each loop onto the turned edge 2 times over the index finger (the width of which becomes the size of the loop). Cover each loop tightly with buttonhole stitches. Sew the buttons on the opposite band.

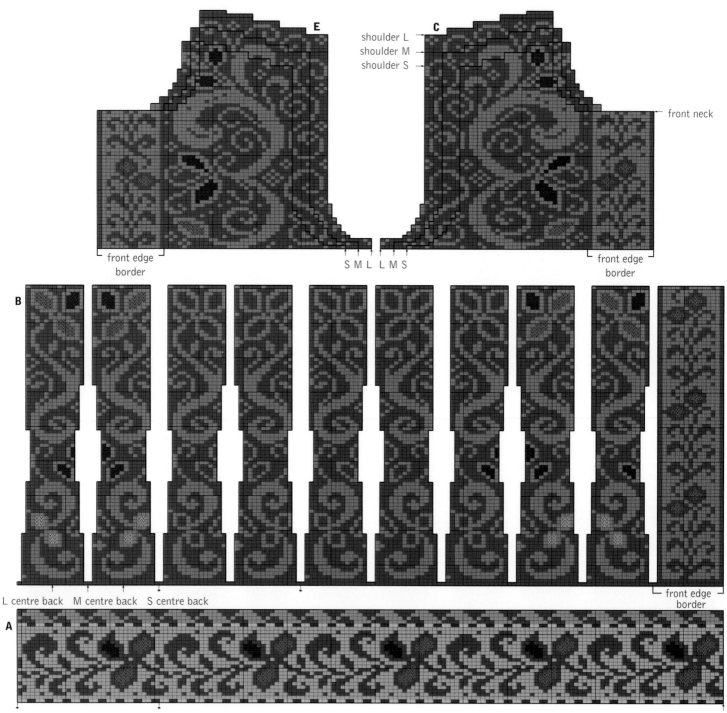

FITTED EMBROIDERED JACKET

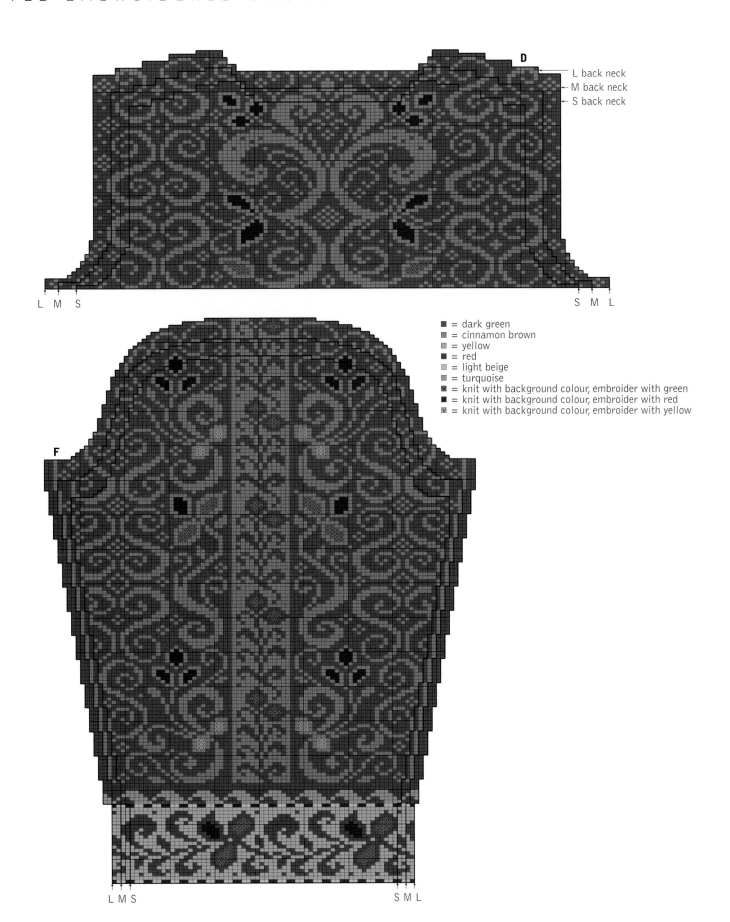

L back neck
M back neck
S back neck

■ = dark green
■ = cinnamon brown
■ = yellow
■ = red
■ = light beige
■ = turquoise
☑ = knit with background colour, embroider with green
■ = knit with background colour, embroider with red
☑ = knit with background colour, embroider with yellow

DESIGNER'S BACKGROUND AND INSPIRATION

Betty Hermansen
Born in 1942 in Bergen.

Education
Certificate in embroidery from Soest in Germany.
Bergen Art-Handicraft School, Textile Program.

Professional Work
Betty has had extensive experience in drawing and design, from Husfliden (Norwegian Handicraft Association) and TEKO in Bergen to church textiles and the sports chapel at Finse. Working out of her own studio, she designs and produces knitted clothing as well as handknitting designs for Rauma Ullvarefabrikk, Husfliden in Bergen and Dale of Norway. From 1989 to 1994, she collaborated with Per Spook in the development of knitted patterns for Haute Couture, working from his idea sketches. She also produced knitted garments which sold in his Paris boutique.

Betty has won several prizes for her designs, in Germany as well as other places. She has also participated in several exhibitions, including the 1997 Norwegian Handicraft and Culture Exposition in Bergen.

JACKET WITH HAT

The jacket is knitted in the round and cut open for the centre front and armholes afterwards. The borders along the front opening are knitted with the body but the facings are added afterwards. The model is knitted in one size only, with a choice of two sleeve lengths.

SIZE
One size
Total circumference:	56 3/4in	144cm
Total length:	33 1/2in	85cm
Underarm length M	13 1/2in	34cm
Underarm length L/XL	16 1/2in	42cm

MATERIALS
Vestland yarn (100% pure new wool – 100 metres per 50 g) from Gjestal Spinneri:
blue (206)	800 g
dark mustard (245)	1000 g

+ 100 g blue and 50 g dark mustard for the hat.
Needles: circular and dpn 4 and 6 (3.5 and 4mm), plus circular ndl 2 (3mm).
Notions/haberdashery: an oblong wooden button, about 2"/5cm long.
Gauge/tension: 22 sts and 26 rows = 4 x 4in/10 x 10cm in pattern on ndls 6 (4mm).
Be sure that your gauge is correct! Change to larger or smaller needles if necessary.

JACKET
Pattern
Chart A shows the right front and half of the back; chart B shows the entire sleeve. On the body, the pattern is reversed from the centre back. The sizes on the sleeve are marked with arrows and dark lines. Follow the arrows and marking lines for the sleeve size you have chosen.

Body
With blue and circular ndl 4 (3.5mm), CO 365 sts. The yarn for the cast-on will be removed when the facing is knitted. Change to dark mustard and knit 3 rows back and forth (the 2nd row will be the turning). CO 4 new sts at the centre front; join and knit in the round. The new sts + 1 st on each side (= 6 sts) are tightly knitted in «lice» pattern for the centre front steek. Change to ndl 6 (4mm). Knit the pattern following chart A, starting at the 3rd row (the first 2 rows have already been worked). Begin at the right side of the chart after the steek sts and reverse the pattern from the centre st. At the arrows marking the neck and armholes, work as follows: Knit the front border over 24 sts, K2tog, work the main pattern over 43 sts, knit the following 55 sts with mustard and cut yarn. Place these 55 sts on a holder for the armhole and CO 6 new sts over the bound-off sts for the steek. Knit the main pattern over 115 sts, knit 55 sts with mustard and cut yarn. Set these 55 sts on a holder and CO 6 new sts over the bound-off sts for the steek. Knit the main pattern over 43 sts, K2tog tbl; work the front border over the last 24 sts, then the 6 steek sts. Continue working in the round following the chart. The armhole steek is tightly knitted in a 'lice' pattern (see Embroidery on page 5) for the whole length. Repeat the decs on each side of the front border every 8th rnd 5 times and then every 6th rnd 6 times. At the arrow for the shoulder, place all the sts, except for the front border sts, on a holder. Divide these 24 sts for the right front border + the 6 steek sts + the 24 left front border sts onto dpn 6 (4mm) and CO 6 new sts for the steek between the borders. Continue knitting in the round, following the chart for the border with all the steek sts in tight lice pattern.
When you bind off for the neck on the front borders, begin working back and forth. Knit to the side which will be bound off until there are 4 pattern sts left; turn, sl 1 st and work to the opposite side until 4 pattern sts remain. *Turn, sl 1 st and work to the opposite side until there are 3 sts left before the last turning; repeat from * until there are 5 pattern sts remaining on each side. Place all the sts on a holder.

Sleeves
Sizes M (L/XL)
With mustard and ndl 4 (3.5mm), CO 131 (131) sts; join. Knit 24 rnds in stockinette for the facing. At the same time, dec 1 st on each side of the 2 centre sts at the underarm every 4th rnd until there are 123 sts on the ndl. Purl 1 rnd for the turning and then continue in stockinette, working 1 rnd in mustard and 2 rnds in blue. Change to ndl 6 (4mm) and continue in pattern following chart B from the 5th rnd (the first 4 rnds have already been worked). The first and last sts on each rnd are not worked in pattern but always knitted with mustard. Inc 1 st on each side of the two centre underarm sts – size M: every 4th rnd 7 times and then every 3rd rnd 20 times – 177 sts; size L/XL: every 4th rnd 27 times = 177 sts. When the incs have been completed, CO 4 new sts between the two centre underarm sts. The 4 new sts + 1 st on each side (= 6 sts) are the steek sts and are knitted tightly in lice pattern. Continue knitting in the round following the chart. Finish the main pattern at the arrow marked M for the smaller size. Work the top border (the last 24 rnds of the pattern) on both sizes. Continue with mustard only and knit 1 rnd then work 6 rows back and forth in stockinette with the wrong side outward for the facing. BO loosely.

Finishing
Machine-stitch two lines on each side of the centre of the steeks on the centre front, armholes, between the neck borders and sleeve caps. Cut open between the seams and lightly steam the pieces. Weave the shoulders together with blue yarn and kitchener stitch. Sew the front borders and collar together with kitchener stitch in both colours. Baste a line for the back neckline: mark a curved line about 8 rows deep at the centre back. Machine-stitch a double line along the basting and cut away the extra fabric. Sew the collar to the back neck.
Facing: Remove the cast-on yarn on the body and place all the sts on a circular ndl 4 (3.5mm). Work in stockinette back and forth with mustard. On the first row, dec to 339 sts evenly spaced as follows: K31, K2tog *K10, K2tog; repeat from * a total of 25 times and finish the row. Work 23 rows in stockinette. On the next row, K25 and place these sts on a holder. BO the next 289 sts. Work the facing back and forth in stockinette over the last 25 sts – a total of 264 rows from the turning = to the neck decs on the front borders. Shape the neck so that it matches the front borders as follows: Work to the side where the decreases will be placed until 4 sts remain; turn; sl 1 and work back. *Work to the last 3 sts before the previous turning; turn, sl 1 and work back; repeat from * until 6 sts remain. Work 1 row over all 25 sts and place them on a holder. Pick up 25 sts on the opposite side and work the facing in the same way but in reverse. Weave the facings together at the centre back of the neck with kitchener stitch.
Sew the facings together at the front edges from the right side – sew with mattress stitch with the needle going under 2 cross threads between the light stripes and steek sts on the front edge and 2 cross threads before the edge sts on the facing but work under 3 cross threads on the facing about every 13th time (translator's note: the cross threads are the horizontal threads between the stitches). When there are 32 rows remaining on the front border of the body alternately work 2 and 3 crossed threads on the facing – so that the seam at the centre back on the facing and front edge meet evenly. Steam the facing and seams and loosely sew down the facing on the inside of the body.
Work the facing over the 55 sts you set aside for the armhole with mustard as follows: Work 6 rows in stockinette with the right side out over the first 28 sts and BO loosely. Work the facing over the remaining 27 sts in the same way. Sew the sleeves from the right side and sew the facing loosely over the steek edges on the wrong side.
Sew an oblong wooden button about 18 1/2in/47cm from the turning edge on the left front on the inner light stripe of the front border. Sew a loop on the inside of the right front in the 2nd stitch row from the seam in the front edge over 8 rows. The front borders should overlap each other when the jacket is buttoned.

JACKET WITH HAT

HAT

Pattern

Chart C shows the border pattern for the cuff.

Crown: With mustard and ndl 2 (3mm), CO 112 sts (the cast-on yarn will be removed when the edging is knitted). Change to blue and work stockinette in the round. After completing 16 rnds, place a marker at the beginning of the rnd and after every 28th st around = 4 markers. Begin decreasing for the crown on the next rnd: *K1, K2tog, knit until 3 sts before the next marker, K2tog tbl, K1; repeat from * around (= 8 decreases). Dec in the same way every 4th rnd a total of 3 times; every 3rd rnd 2 times and then every other rnd until 8 sts remain. Knit 8 rnds. Cut yarn and thread tail through remaining sts and fasten on inside.

Edge: Remove the cast-on yarn and place the sts on ndl 4 (3.5mm). Turn the crown so that the wrong side is facing and work 8 rnds in stockinette in the round with blue. Change to mustard and knit 1 rnd. Change to ndl 2 (3mm) and purl 1 rnd for the turning. Change to ndl 4 (3.5mm) and continue in stockinette – knit 1 rnd mustard and 2 rnds blue, increasing 4 sts evenly spaced on the first blue rnd = 116 sts. Change to ndl 6 (4mm) and work border pattern C: begin at the right side of the chart, knit the first 4 sts (the first st = centre back), repeat the section *–* a total of 4 times; knit the next 21 sts (= centre front), work the next repeat *–* a total of 4 times, and then work the last 3 sts in pattern. When the border pattern has been completed, change to ndl 4 (3.5mm) and knit 1 rnd blue. On the next rnd, inc 6 sts evenly spaced around = 122 sts. Place a marker at the centre back and centre front sts and one at each side – 30 sts from the centre back.

Knit another 5 rnds with blue. Then work each short-row section separately, back and forth in stockinette. Knit the front section first: beginning at the centre back st, K 82 sts (there are 10 sts left before the side marker). *Turn, sl 1, work 40 sts back (until 10 sts remain before the next side marker); turn, sl 1, work 35 sts. Turn, sl 1, work 30 sts back. Turn, sl 1, work 25 sts. Turn, sl 1, work 20 sts. Turn, sl 1, work 15 sts. Turn, sl 1, work 10 sts. * Turn, sl 1, work across the centre front st, across to the side marker and to the centre back st until there are 10 sts remaining before the next side marker = a total of 86 sts. Work the back short-row section as for the front short-row section from *–*. Then turn, sl 1, work across the centre back st, across to the side marker and then across the centre front st and to the other side marker, across to the centre back st and to the next side marker = a total of 172 sts. Continue working stockinette in the round over all the sts. The rnd begins at the side marker! Change to mustard and knit 2 rnds, but knit the 2nd rnd on ndl 2 (3mm). Purl 1 rnd for the turning.

Facing: Change to blue for the facing and knit 2 rnds. Work the first short-row section on the front facing: Knit 36 sts from the side marker, *turn, sl 1, work 10 sts back. Turn, sl 1, work 15 sts. Turn, sl 1, work 20 sts. Continue working 5 more sts each time you turn until you have 40 sts.* Turn, sl 1 and work 86 sts. Work the back short-row facing as for the front from *–*. Then turn, sl 1 and work 50 sts to the side marker. Continue working stockinette in the round on ndl 2 (3mm) and dec 6 sts evenly spaced around the first rnd = 116 sts. The facing is complete after a total of 18 rnds from the turning row at the side. BO loosely. Sew the facing to the inside on the lower turning edge. Steam the hat carefully over a hatform.

centre st

B

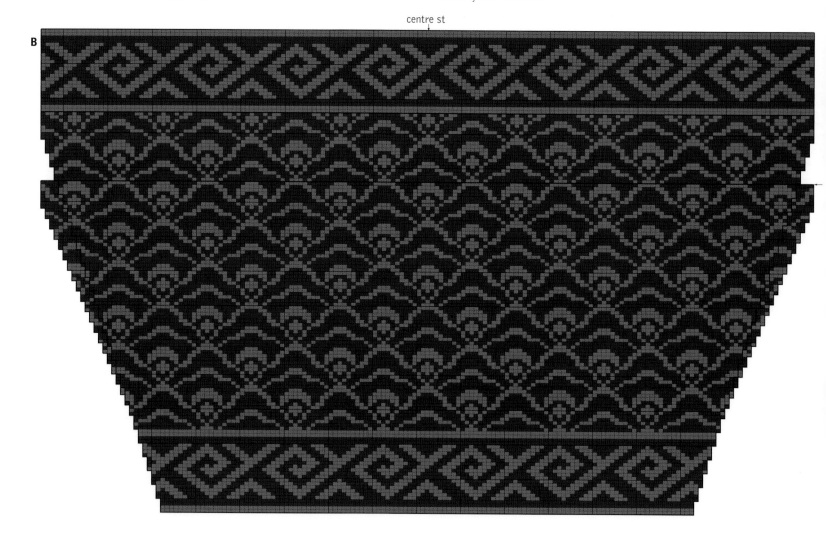

JAKKE MED HATT

JACKET WITH HAT

■ = blue
■ = dark mustard

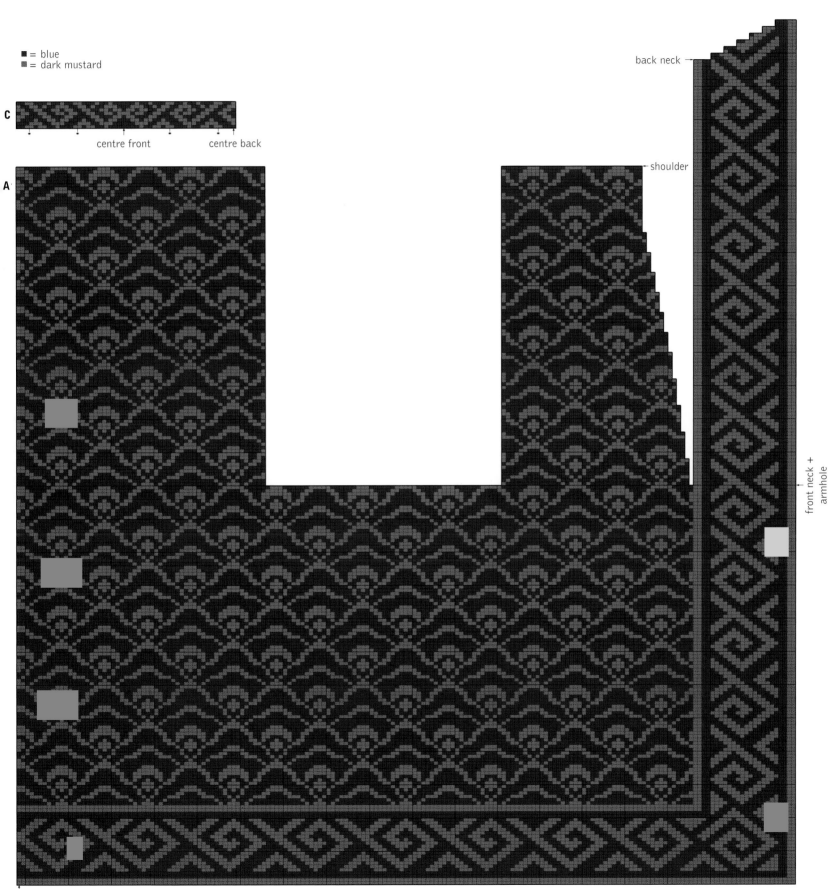

C

centre front   centre back

A

back neck →

→ shoulder

front neck +
armhole

centre back

SHORT JACKET WITH HAT

The jacket is knitted in the round and cut open for the centre front and armholes. The jacket facing is knitted on afterwards and the collar is knitted in Shaker ribbing.

SIZES
S (M) L

Total circumference:	45 3/4 (45 3/4) 50 1/2in
	116 (116) 128cm
Total length:	24 1/2 (26 3/4) 29 1/4in
	62 (68) 74cm
Underarm length:	19 1/4 (21 1/2) 19 1/4in
	49 (55) 49cm

MATERIALS
Pt4 (100% pure new wool – 100 metres per 50 g) from Rauma Ullvarefabrikk (PT-Design):

red (440)	700 (750) 800 g
blue (476)	450 (500) 550 g
green (492)	100 (100) 100 g
yellow (416)	300 (300) 350 g

+ 100 g blue and 50 g red for the hat.
Needles: circular and dpn 4 (3.5mm) and 6 (4mm), plus a short circular ndl 2 (3mm).
Notions/haberdashery: 1 oblong button; the silver button shown in the photo is made by Per Vigeland.
Gauge/tension: 23 sts and 26 rows = 4 x 4in/10 x 10cm in pattern on ndl 6 (4mm).
Be sure that your gauge is correct! Change to larger or smaller needles if necessary.

JACKET
Pattern
Chart A shows the right front and half of the back; chart B shows the entire sleeve. The sizes are marked on the charts with arrows and dark lines. Follow the arrows and marking lines for your size. On the body the pattern repeat is marked between asterisks (*–*), but the motif is reversed starting at the centre back.

Body
With blue and ndl 4 (3.5mm), CO 296 (296) 324 sts (the cast-on thread will be removed when the facing is knitted). Change to red and knit 2 rows, working back and forth (the 2nd row will be the turning row). Change to ndl 6 (4mm) and work the pattern following chart A – the first and last st on the ndl are the edge sts and not worked in pattern; repeat from *–* around. After the first row of the pattern, CO 4 new sts at the centre front and work in the round. The edge sts and the 4 new sts (= 6 sts) are always knitted tightly in lice pattern for the entire length and form the centre front steek.
At the arrow for the armhole, work as follows: knit the pattern across 70 (70) 84 sts (= right front); knit the next 28 (28) 14 sts with red and place these sts on a holder. Cut yarn and CO 6 new sts over the bound-off sts for the armhole steek. Knit the pattern across the next 98 (98) 126 sts (= back); knit the next 28 (28) 14 sts with red and place these sts on a holder. Cut yarn and CO 6 new sts over the bound-off sts for the armhole steek; finish knitting the pattern across the last 70 (70) 84 sts (= left front) + the 6 steek sts. Continue working in the round.
The armhole steeks are knitted tightly in lice pattern for the entire length. At the arrow for the neckline, work as follows: Knit the first 28 sts with red, knit the pattern until there are 28 sts left on the rnd (not including the steek sts); knit the last 28 sts with red. Place the steek sts + 28 sts on each side of the steek on a holder. CO 6 new sts over the bound-off sts for the steek and continue working in the round following the chart. After knitting another block (a total of 8 (9) 9 blocks from the turning edge), knit 14 sts with red, knit the pattern

until 14 sts remain on the rnd and knit these with red. Place the steek sts + 14 sts at each side of the steek on a holder. CO 6 new steek sts over the bound-off sts and continue working in the round to the arrow marking the shoulder (= a total of 10 (11) 12 blocks from the turning). Place all the sts on a holder.

Finishing
Machine-stitch 2 lines on each side of the centre front and armhole steeks. Cut open between the lines and carefully steam the pieces.

Facing and Collar
Remove the cast-on yarn from the body and place all 296 (296) 324 sts on circular ndl 4 (3.5mm). Work in stockinette back and forth with red but dec evenly on the first row to 280 (280) 305 sts: Knit 44 (44) 38 sts, *K2tog, K 11; repeat from * a total of 16 (16) 19 times and finish the row. Work a total of 20 rows. On the next row, work 43 sts and place them on a holder for the front edge facing; BO the next 194 (194) 219 sts and work the last 43 sts. Continue working the front edge facing back and forth across these 43 sts. Work until the facing reaches the first sts which were set aside for the neck (= about 130 (150) 150 rows from the turning row). Before you continue with the collar, the facing must be sewn together with the body: Insert the ndl between the edge sts and the pattern sts in the 2nd row at the bottom on the body. Right side facing, with mattress stitch, alternately insert the needle under 2 cross threads from the facing (before the edge st) and 2 cross threads from the body, but, about every 3rd time, use 3 crossed threads from the facing, so that it doesn't pull in. The cross threads are the horizontal threads between the stiches. Sew it all the way up. Knit the 28 sts from the facing together with the 28 set-aside sts from the body by drawing 1 st from the facing through 1 st from the body, 2 sts from the facing through 2 sts from the body, etc. Continue in Shaker ribbing for the collar over the 28 sts and stockinette for the facing over the 14 remaining sts – a total of 24 rows.
Shaker ribbing: K1, P1 on both the right and wrong sides, but for each row on the right side, work knit sts in the st below.
Sew the facings together with the body as follows: Using mattress stitch, sew, alternately, 2 cross threads from the body and 3 cross threads between the collar ribbing and stockinette all the way up. Work the 14 sts in stockinette from the facing together with the 14 single colours sts from the body in the same way as previously. CO 6 new sts for the facing in towards the body and continue with the Shaker ribbing over 42 sts and stockinette over the 6 facing sts. Work another 88 (88) 106 rows. Finish the collar: Work 1 row from the facing side, work back until 5 ribbing and 6 facing sts remain, *turn, sl 1, finish the row and then work back until 4 sts remain before the last turning – repeat from * until there are 9 ribbing sts left. Work 1 row over all 48 sts and place them on a holder. (= centre back neck). Work the other facing and collar in the same way but in reverse.
The collar pieces and then the shoulders are sewn together with red yarn. Mark a curved line for the back neck so that it is about 6 rows deep at the centre back and baste. Machine-stitch a double line along the basting and cut away the extra fabric.
Sew the collar to the body by inserting the needle under 2 cross threads from the body and 3 cross threads between the ribbing and stockinette up to the shoulder seam.
Sew the collar to the neck on the back and sew the facing over the raw edges on the wrong side. Turn the collar in and sew it down to the neck back, about 4in/10cm out to each side from the centre back. Work the facings at the base of the arm openings, using the 28 (28) 14 sts in red. Divide the sts in half and work 6 rows in stockinette over 14 (14) 7 sts. BO loosely. Work a similar facing with the rest of the sts.

SHORT JACKET WITH HAT

Sleeves

With red and ndl 4 (3.5mm), CO 66 (66) 72 sts; join. Knit 20 rnds in stockinette for the facing, decreasing 1 st at each side of the 2 centre sts at the underarm every 4th rnd until there are 58 (58) 64 sts on the ndl. Purl 1 rnd for the turning. Change to ndl 6 (4mm) and work the pattern following chart B – the first and last sts on the rnd are not drawn on the chart – these are always worked without patterning in the pattern colour of the nearest block (which means that the sts will be in different colours). Knit the sts between the arrows for your size. Inc 1 st on each side of the 2 centre underarm sts – size S: every 4th rnd until there are 114 sts on the ndl and the sleeve is 7 blocks high; size M: every 5th rnd 13 times and then every 4th rnd until there are 114 sts on the ndl and the sleeve is 8 blocks high; size L: every 3rd rnd until there are 142 sts on the ndl and the sleeve is 7 1/2 blocks high.

CO 4 new sts between the centre underarm sts – the 2 centre sts + these 4 sts are tightly knitted in lice pattern for the steek. Continue knitting to the arrow for your size = 8 (9) 8 blocks high (size L has shorter sleeves than size M, because the drop shoulders extend down further). Finish with red – knit 1 rnd. Change to ndl 4 (3.5) and purl 6 rnds for the facing. BO loosely.

Finishing: Steam the sleeves lightly. Machine-stitch 2 lines on each side of the centre of the 4 steek sts at the top of the sleeve and cut open between them. Sew the sleeves in on the right side – make sure that the blocks meet evenly. Sew the facing over the raw edges on the wrong side. Sew a loop (long enough for the button) on the right front, in the edge of the border under the collar. Sew a button securely on the left front so that the 2 blocks overlap each other when the jacket is buttoned.

HAT

Facing: With red and circular ndl 4 (3.5mm), CO 118 sts; join. Knit stockinette in the round. On the 4th rnd, inc 4 sts as follows (the beginning of the rnd = centre back): K28, inc 1, K2 and place a marker between these 2 sts (= side marker); inc 1, K29 and place a marker (= centre front); K29, inc 1, K2 and place a marker between these 2 sts (= side marker); inc 1 and K 28 = rnd finished. Knit 3 rnds. Dec 1 st on each side of the 2 centre back sts every 3rd rnd a total of 5 times: K1, K2tog, knit until 3 sts left on the rnd, K2tog tbl, K1. At the same time, continue increasing at each side on every 3rd rnd until you have increased a total of 5 times. After the last centre back dec, knit 3 rnds over the 128 sts on the ndl. Continue with short rows at the lower edge of the facing working each side separately, back and forth in stockinette.

Begin the short rows at the side as follows: **NOTE:** sl 1 at the beginning of each row every time you turn and then work the specified number of sts.) K46, turn and P41; turn and K38; turn and P33; turn and K30; turn and P25; turn and K22; turn and P17; turn and K14; turn and P10; turn and K7; turn and P3; turn and K48.

Centre front short rows: **NOTE:** sl 1 at the beginning of the row every time you turn and then work the specified number of sts.) Turn and P23; turn and K20; turn and P17; turn and K14; turn and P11; turn and K8; turn and P5; turn and K62.

Then knit the short rows on the other side: **NOTE:** sl 1 at the beginning of the row every time you turn and then work the specified number of sts. Turn and P41; turn and K36; turn and P33; turn and K28; turn and P25; turn and K20; turn and P17; turn and K13; turn and P10; turn and K6; turn and P3; turn and K30 = end of rnd. Knit 1 rnd across all the sts, increasing at the same time 1 st on each side of the 2 centre back sts = 130 sts on the ndl.

Crown: Change to ndl 2 (3mm) and purl 1 rnd for the turning. Change to ndl 4 (3.5mm) and continue in stockinette with blue. Knit 1 rnd + 32 sts on the next rnd. Work the short rows at the side: **NOTE:** sl 1 at the beginning of the row every time you turn and then work the specified number of sts. Turn and P3; turn and K6; turn and P10; turn and K13; turn and P17; turn and K20; turn and P25; turn and K28; turn and P33; turn and K36; turn and P41; turn and K62.

Next work the centre front short rows: **NOTE:** sl 1 at the beginning of the row every time you turn and then work the specified number of sts. Turn and P5; turn and K8; turn and P11; turn and K14; turn and P17; turn and K20; turn and P23; turn and K48.

Short rows on the other side: **NOTE:** sl 1 at the beginning of the row every time you turn and then work the specified number of sts. Turn and P3; turn and K7; turn and P10; turn and K14; turn and P17; turn and K22; turn and P25; turn and K30; turn and P33; turn and K38; turn and P41; turn and K46 = end of rnd. Knit 3 rnds over all the sts. Inc 1 st on each side of the 2 centre back sts on the next rnd. Knit 3 rnds. Next rnd: K1, inc 1, K27, K2tog tbl, K2 and place a marker between these 2 sts (= side marker), K2tog, K64, K2tog tbl, K2 and place a marker between these two sts (= side marker); K2tog, K27, inc 1, K1. Knit 3 rnds. Repeat these increases/decreases every 4th rnd another 3 times – there will be 2 fewer sts at the centre front between the decreases each time. Stop increasing at the centre back, but continue decreasing in the same way at each side of the side markers on every 4th rnd 3 times – there will be 1 st less on the first dec, 2 fewer sts at the centre front and 1 st less on the last dec each time. K 4 rnds, dec in the same way on the next rnd. Knit 4 rnds.

Divide the sts onto four dpn, starting at the centre back, with 27 sts on each  ndl. *K1, K2tog, K21, K2tog tbl, K1; repeat from * on each ndl around (= 8 decs). Knit 3 rnds. Dec in the same way every 4th rnd until 76 sts remain. There will be 2 fewer sts between decs each time. Knit 2 rnds. Continue decreasing on every other rnd until 5 sts remain on each ndl. Knit 2 rnds. Dec on the next rnd: K2tog, K1, K2tog tbl; repeat from * around. Knit 5 rnds with the remaining 12 sts for the top. Change to red and knit 1 rnd, purl 1 rnd, knit 1 rnd. K2, K2tog around on next rnd.

Cut yarn and thread tail through remaining sts and fasten on inside. Steam hat and sew the facing loosely on the wrong side.

BETTY HERMANSEN

SHORT JACKET WITH HAT

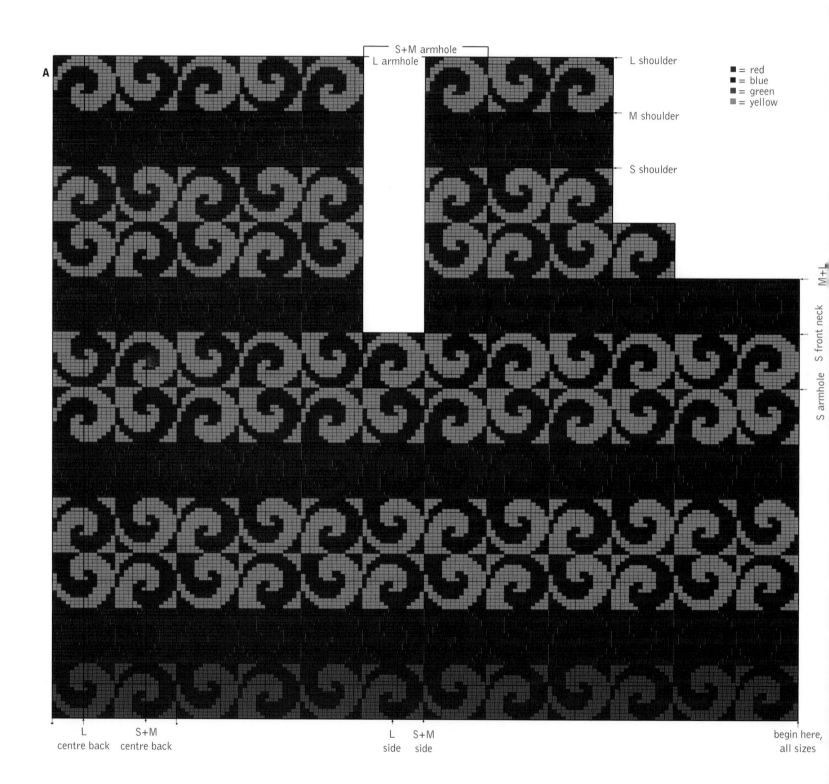

A

S+M armhole
L armhole

L shoulder

M shoulder

S shoulder

■ = red
■ = blue
■ = green
■ = yellow

M+L

S front neck

S armhole

L
centre back

S+M
centre back

L
side

S+M
side

begin here,
all sizes

SHORT JACKET WITH HAT

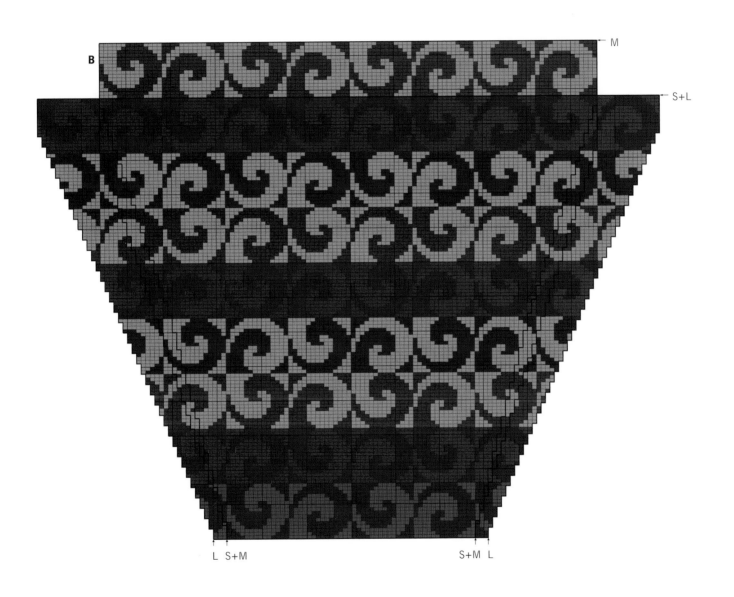

DESIGNER'S BACKGROUND AND INSPIRATION

Margaretha Finseth
Born in 1954.

Education
Seven year's technical training in dress and costume sewing and weaving. Trained in weaving at the Technical School in Oslo, Esthetics Department.

Professional Work
Margaretha has worked in the production of handwoven ecclesiastical textiles, damask, costume textiles and reconstruction of old textiles at the Norwegian Handicraft Association's Weaving Workshop in Oslo.
In 1983, she began to work with knitting design. Since 1985, she has had her own company which sells design services for hand- and machine-knitting and she has worked in Norway, Sweden and Denmark. She has developed special designs for a number of booklets and magazines, and was employed as the designer for the monthly magazine, Fashion Journal from 1994–95. Since 1986, she has worked as a freelance journalist, writing articles on design, lifestyle and trends, interior, fashion, health and well-being for weekly and monthly magazines, such as The New, Fashion Journal, Women & Clothing, and Hers. She has also worked for many years as the stylist and make-up artist for fashion magazines, catalogue production and advertising companies and was responsible for the direction and choreography of several fashion shows.
In 1989–90, she was engaged by NORAD/Norimpod in a women's handknitting project in Nepal and was responsible for design, instructor training, technical planning, and production of handknitted garments for sale in the West. She also developed the collection's graphic profile and logo: ATTITUDE Knitting – by women for women.
In 1992, she worked in Kathmandu, Nepal as a consultant for the company, House of Rajkarnicar, establishing a textile export conference. Her responsibilities included directing fashion shows during the conference and courses and guidance for Nepalese designers considering clothing for the export market to the West.
She resumed the work in Nepal in 1998, producing a collection of ecological handknitted clothing in pure wool.
Margaretha has been retained as an consultant/lecturer on themes and trends, establishing decentralized production on workshop principles, design strategies and concept development for small concerns within the textile industry. Later she worked on design projects for several Norwegian TEKO concerns.

Executive Work
Since 1993, Margaretha has been active in administration in the Norwegian Textile and Decorative Designers, NTKD and was a leader during 1998-99. Through Norwegian Form – Centre for Design, Architecture and Building Environment, she has been involved in establishing the Designers' Fall Exhibition, 'FORM '96' and 'FORM '98'; served as TEKO-representative in the Norwegian Form Council in 1997–99 as well as in the jury for the Norwegian Design Council's section of 'The Mark for Good Design' in 1998. In 1999, she was on the board of the Norwegian Textile Council, serving as designer-representative. Margaretha is especially involved in design adaptions which are ecological and which meet resource and environmental goals. She has written articles on the material, including legal goals tied to designers' authorial and contractual rights.

Awards
1st prize for design of the official ski sweater for Norway's Ski Association 1994 Winter Olympics at Lillehammer. The sweater, 'Lillehammer' was chosen by Norway's Olympic committee for the Norwegian Olympic team's official parade outfit at the same games. The sweater was produced by Dale of Norway.

On Designing
- It is the 'inner soul' of Norwegian wool and handknitting which inspires me in my work with handknitting design. I think about the endless possibilities which lie in handwork for creating unique textiles in patterns, colours and shapes with which one can create three-dimensional forms totally without seams and joins.

Folk art and folk costumes drive the creative process. Besides my own Norwegian cultural heritage, and not least my roots in northern Norway's culture, are the Ur-cultures from Gaia's northern hemisphere with which I feel a relationship in regards to form. This includes, for example, the Inuit, west-Siberian and Mongolian indigenous people's traditional garments, but also Japanese and Chinese traditional clothing. It isn't always materials and ornaments but, perhaps more often, the decorative elements which are fascinating. I wonder over these simple, geometric forms which build garments as one raises architectural structures. At the same time, I have a deep respect for the ecological where man uses resources optimally and, for the most part, uses local raw materials. The result is functional and beautiful garments with the strength and quality to withstand use for generations.

- By going back to traditional textiles and folk art, one can find the original and perhaps actual necessities. It must be a meaningful goal in itself to consider consumer society's relationship with clothing and textiles. When one puts so much time and soul into a handknitted garment, the result ought to overcome fashionable modes and the use-and-toss mentality. It is the starting point for creating garments which have their own worth irregardless of trends and skirt lengths. It is precisely that which is simple, clean, practical and appropriate in combination with creative needs and a fruitful language of form which characterizes indigenous people's way of clothing themselves and which connects to my own considerations about clothing.

THE DARKNESS AND LIGHT OF WINTER

The jacket is knitted in two different yarns. The lower border, front- and sleeve-bands are knitted back and forth in cable and lace patterns with 3-ply Strikkegarn. The sleeves and body front and back are knitted in the round in a leaf pattern with Finull yarn – from the wrist to the centre front and from and back to the centre back. The two parts are knitted together at the centre back afterwards. The bands on both the body and sleeves are lined with figured velvet.

SIZES

S (M/L)

Total circumference:	47 1/4 (52)in	120 (132)cm
Total length:	16 (18)in	41 (46cm)
Length from wrist to wrist:	64 3/4 (69 1/2)in	164 (176)cm

MATERIALS:

3-ply Strikkegarn (100% pure new wool – 108 metres per 50g) from Rauma Ullvarefabrikk:

charcoal grey (107)	350 (400) g

Finnull yarn (100% pure new wool, about 175 metres per 50 g) from Rauma Ullvarefabrikk:

grey tweed (414)	200 (200) g
grey-blue (447)	200 (200) g

Needles: circular ndls 1 and 4 (2.5 and 3.5mm).

Notions/haberdashery: For the lining on the bands: 27 1/2in/70cm royal blue figured velvet in 60in/150cm width, plus 24in/60cm black iron-on interfacing.

Gauge/tension: with 3-ply Strikkegarn – 23 sts and 26 rows = 4 x 4in/ 10 x 10cm in stockinette on ndl 4 (3.5mm); 30 sts and 32 rows in cable/lace pattern = 4 x 4in/10 x 10cm on ndl 4 (3.5mm).

With Finull yarn – 30 sts and 33 rows = 4 x 4in/10 x 10cm in stockinette and leaf pattern on ndl 1 (2.5mm).

Be sure that your gauge is correct! Change to larger or smaller needles if necessary.

PATTERN

Chart A shows the jacket's left side – with the sleeve, one front and half of the back. Chart B shows the pattern repeat for the jacket's right side. Chart C shows the bands for the body – with the lower edge to the centre back and the repeat for the front and collar. The sleeve bands are knitted as for the front bands on chart C.

Left Sleeve, front and back

Begin at the lower edge of the sleeve. With grey tweed Finnull and ndl 1 (2.5mm), CO 168 (180) sts; join. Working in the round, knit 2 rnds. Continue with the pattern following chart A: K1 with grey tweed; begin at the arrow for your size on the right side of the chart and knit to the arrow on the left side; finish with K1 grey tweed. The 2 sts at the underarm are knitted with grey tweed without

patterning for the entire length. Dec 1 st at each side of the 2 centre underarm sts every 10 (11) rnds 12 times = 144 (156) sts remaining. When the work measures 15 (16)in/38 (41cm), CO 4 new sts at the underarm for the steek for the lower part of the body and continue working in the round, following the chart. The steek sts are worked without patterning for the entire length. When the piece measures 21 1/4 (23 5/8)in/ 54 (60)cm, BO the 4 steek sts. Leave the first 72 (78) sts on the ndl for the back, while working 2 rows in stockinette with grey tweed over the last 72 (78) sts for the front. Then BO these sts = centre front. Continue, working back and forth and following the chart across the 72 (78) sts for the back until the piece measures 26 3/4 (29 1/4)in/68 (74)cm from the cast-on row. Work 2 rows in stockinette with grey tweed, place the sts on a holder and put aside.

Right sleeve, front and back: CO and work as for the left side of the jacket but with the pattern in reverse – chart B shows the reversed pattern repeat. Begin at the arrow for your size at the lower edge of the sleeve.

Machine-stitch 2 lines on each side of the centre of the 4 steek sts at the lower edge of the body and cut between the lines.

With grey tweed and right sides facing each other, weave the two back pieces together with a 3 needle bind-off with P2 tog.

Lower band, Front bands and Collar: with 3-ply Strikkegarn, and ndl 4 (3.5mm), CO 282 (308) sts; join. The first 7 and last 7 sts on the row (14 sts) are used for the facing and the centre front steek. Working in the round, knit 10 rnds for the facing and an eyelet row for the turning – *K2tog tbl, yo; repeat from * around but not over the 14 facing and centre front steek sts. Then knit 1 rnd, increasing 80 (90) sts evenly spaced around (about every 3rd st) but do not inc over the 14 facing and steek sts = 348 (384) sts for the cable and lace pattern + 14 facing and centre front steek sts. Continue, following chart C – begin with K2 = steek, work from the right side of the chart (the first 5 sts = facing/cable); repeat the section from *–* until 7 sts remain; finish with 5 facing sts/cable and K2 = steek.

Knit to the arrow for your size = 55 (67) rnds. BO the 4 centre front steek sts and place 47 sts on each side of these on a holder = 42 sts for the front + 5 facing sts on each side. To reduce the width, work K2, K2tog across all the cable sts on the next row. BO these sts on the next row.

Work each front band separately back and forth, following the chart, repeat *–* until it reaches the centre back neck when the piece is slightly stretched = about 9 1/2 (10 1/4)in/24 (26)cm for the front band + about 8in/20cm for the collar. Place these sts on a holder until the other side is completed. Machine-stitch and cut the centre front as for the lower edge of the body. Place the collar sections right sides facing each other and work 3 ndl bind-off with P2tog.

Sleeve bands

With 3-ply Strikkegarn and ndl 4 (3.5)mm, CO 47 sts. Work the cable/lace pattern back and forth as for the front bands on chart C – begin at the arrow for the sleeve edging, with the 1st row on the wrong side = 42 sts for the sleeve edging + 5 sts for the facing/cable. Repeat *–* until the piece is long enough to go around the end of the sleeve = about 22 (23 5/8)in/56 (60)cm. BO. Work the other band in reverse so that the bands will look alike when assembled.

Finishing

Dip and squeeze the pieces in about about 2.5 gal/10 liters warm water with 1 capful neutral soap. Rinse 2–3 times and then put the pieces in a pillow case or nylon washing bag and centrifuge or spin. Lightly stretch the pieces to measurements and lay flat to dry. Lightly steam the pieces on the wrong side under a damp cloth. Be extra careful with the cable-knitted pieces so that the cables don't flatten. Do not press the iron against the pieces but hold it slightly above the cloth and let the steam seep through the cloth and knitted pieces as you move over each piece.

Using the cable/lace pieces for measurements, make a paper pattern for the lining. Add about 5/8in/1.5cm for the seams and cut out the lining in figured velvet. Iron interfacing along the lining's front edges, from the eyelet row down to the centre back neck – the rest of the jacket's lower edges as well as the sleeve edges are not interfaced.

Turn the facing for the body's lower edge to the inside and sew on the wrong side.

Turn the cable facings along the front edges and collar to the wrong side and sew.

Join the short sides of the sleeve edges; turn the cable facing down on the sleeve edge to the wrong side and sew.

Join the whole edging to the body from the right side with mattress st – sew by stitching into the edge sts alternately on the body and edging, working carefully so that the seam does not draw in and pucker. The front edges go over the collar which is sewn to the back.

Join the sleeve edges with mattress st.

Fitting the lining: turn in the seam and pin it down. Sew first along the outer edges – the lining is sewn along the front edge/collar to the edge st before the cable facing. Then sew the inner edge, so that the lining covers all the seams on the garment's pieces. Sew the lining to the edges of the sleeves in the same way.

THE DARKNESS AND LIGHT OF WINTER

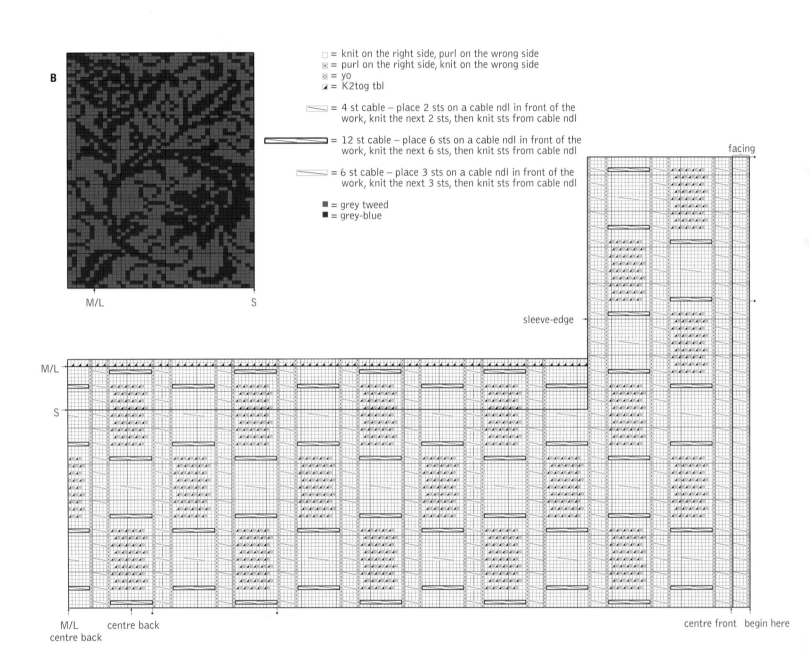

B

□ = knit on the right side, purl on the wrong side
⊠ = purl on the right side, knit on the wrong side
⊙ = yo
◪ = K2tog tbl

= 4 st cable – place 2 sts on a cable ndl in front of the work, knit the next 2 sts, then knit sts from cable ndl

= 12 st cable – place 6 sts on a cable ndl in front of the work, knit the next 6 sts, then knit sts from cable ndl

= 6 st cable – place 3 sts on a cable ndl in front of the work, knit the next 3 sts, then knit sts from cable ndl

■ = grey tweed
■ = grey-blue

M/L

S

facing

sleeve-edge

M/L

S

M/L
centre back

centre back

centre front   begin here

M/L
centre back

THE DARKNESS AND LIGHT OF WINTER

MARGARETHA FINSETH

GREY STONES, WHITE SEA TRADING
AND BOAT RUGS

The coat is knitted back and forth in strips – 4 for the back and 2 each for the fronts. These are joined and then the yoke is knitted in three sections, with the back and front pieces each worked separately. Each sleeve is knitted in the round up to the sleeve cap, which is worked back and forth. The looped bands at the lower edge of the coat and sleeves as well as the detached collar are crocheted with a mohair yarn, Trollgarn, and Hifa 3. The looped bands, detached collar, front edges and collar are lined with black cotton velvet.

SIZE
M/L

Total Circumference:	39 1/2in	100cm
Total length:	52 3/4in	134cm + looped band
Underarm length:	19 3/4in	50cm + looped band
Lower width:		79in	200cm

MATERIALS
Hifa Trollgarn (100% pure new wool – 114 metres per 100 g) from Hillesvåg Ullvarefabrikk:

grey (704)   3800 g

Hifa 3 Strikkegarn-knitting yarn (100% pure new wool – 210 metres per 100 g) from Hillesvåg Ullvarefabrikk:

charcoal grey (6056)   150 g for the looped bands
grey tweed (6061)   50 g for the finishing

Long-hair mohair yarn (at least 75% mohair):
         450 g grey tweed and 900 g black for the looped bands.
Needles: long and short circular ndls 7 (4.5mm), a cable ndl, and crochet hooks G and H (4 and 5mm).
Notions/haberdashery: 3 plain buttons, 1 1/2in/3.8cm in diametre for the backing of the crocheted buttons, + 8 small fur hooks (4 for the front closure and 4 for the detached collar). Black cotton velvet sufficient for lining the front edges, collar, sleeve edges, lower edge and detached collar + black iron-on interfacing for the collar.
Gauge/tension: Cable/lace in Trollgarn on ndls 7/4.5mm – 1 large cable = about 4in/10cm high and 2 3/8in/6cm wide measured at the centre of the lace pattern. A strip for the body – 9 1/2in/25cm wide at the lower edge, 6 1/4in/16cm wide at the top and 41 3/4in/106cm long. All the measurements are taken on lightly steamed pieces without any stretching/blocking of the pieces.
Be sure that your gauge is correct! Change to larger or smaller ndls if necessary.

PATTERN
Chart A shows a strip for the body in cable/lace pattern. Chart B shows the decreases for the cables at the beginning of the yoke and C shows the rest of the yoke front and back. Chart D shows the pattern for the sleeves.

Back
The back is made with 4 strips.
With Trollgarn and ndl 7 (4.5mm), CO 62 sts for a strip. Work the cable/lace pattern back and forth, following chart A, with the 1st row on the wrong side: Knit 1 edge st, *K1, P4, K1, P12; repeat from * a total of 3 times, ending with K1, P4, K1, + 1 edge st. Follow the chart, working the repeat *–* at the side of the chart a total of 4 times, so that you have a total of 17 cable crossings before the first dec on the cables. **NOTE:** If you wish to shorten the coat, do so before

the decreases. Dec, as explained below, in the cables marked with arrows on the pattern. The chart shows which cables are decreased.
1st and 2nd cables with decs: Place 6 sts on a cable ndl in front of the piece, K2tog tbl twice, K2, then knit the 6 sts from the cable ndl.
3rd and 4th cables with decs: Place 5 sts on a cable ndl in front of the piece, K2tog tbl twice, K1, then knit the 5 sts from the cable ndl.
5th and 6th cables with decs: Place 4 sts on a cable ndl in front of the piece, K2tog tbl twice, sl 1 over the 2nd st then K2 sts from the cable ndl and K2tog tbl with the last 2 sts on the cable ndl.
Finish with 1 purl row and set the work aside = 36 sts with 7 small cables.

Fronts
Each front is made with 2 strips. Work the first strip as for the back. For the second strip, CO 69 sts = 62 as for the other strips + 7 sts for the facing at the centre front. The cables on the facing are knitted like the small cables on chart A, with the sts divided this way on the right side: 1 edge st, P1, 4 cable sts, P1. The edge st on the chart which is nearest the facing is purled on the right side and knitted on the wrong side. Be sure that you work the facing sts in reverse order for the other front.

Yokes
Back Yoke: The back has 4 strips of 36 sts each = 144 sts. Sew the strips together on the right side using mattress st and grey tweed Hifa 3. Insert the needle, alternating between each section, into the edge st and draw the pieces together so that they will lie smoothly. The yoke is worked starting on the right side on ndl 7 (4.5mm) and Trollgarn.
1st row: Work the small cables and dec at the centre of each strip as shown on chart B by repeating *–*, but, at the same time, P2 tog with the first and last st of each strip and CO 1 new st at each side for the edge st = 133 sts + 2 edge sts after the first row. The edge sts are knitted on each row and not worked in pattern. After the decs in pattern B are complete, there should be 20 small cables + 2 edge sts = 103 sts. Continue working the small cables following chart C up to the arrow marking the shoulders and neck = about 10 1/4in/26cm for the yoke. BO for the shoulders and neck at the same time by placing the specified number of sts on a holder at the beginning of each row as shown on the chart. Finish with 1 row across the 35 shoulder sts, working K2, K2tog tbl over each cable. BO the shoulder sts on the next row. Place the 33 neck sts on a holder.

Front Yoke: Each front has 1 strip with 36 sts and a strip with 43 sts = 79 sts. Sew the strips together and work following chart B as for the back, but CO 1 edge st at the side edge = 7 facing sts + 67 sts + 1 edge st after the first row. The 7 facing sts are not drawn on the chart but are worked as previously all the way up to the neckline. After working the decs in pattern B, there should be 1 facing cable + 10 small cables + 1 edge st = 59 sts. Continue, working the small cables as on chart C to the arrow marking the neckline = about 8in/20cm for the front yoke. Dec for the neck by placing sts onto a holder at the beginning of each row at the neck edge: first, the 7 facing sts + 5 sts, then as shown on the chart. Keep the 24 sts for the neck on the holder. Shape the shoulders when they are the same length and measurements as on the back. Join the shoulder sts with mattress st and Hifa 3 Strikkegarn.

Sleeves
With Trollgarn and circular ndl 7 (4.5mm), CO 108 sts; join. Work in the round following chart D: begin at the arrow and place a marker where indicated by the arrow at the underarm, moving the marker up as you work. Repeat *–* for the entire length.

GREY STONES, WHITE SEA TRADING

AND BOAT RUGS

When the piece measures 19 3/4in/50cm, begin decreasing for the sleeve cap by removing sts at each side of the underarm marker. Work back and forth at the same time as you move the first 9 sts on the ndl to a holder (use a circular ndl) at the beginning of each row at each side 5 times = 18 sts remaining. Work one row in stockinette over all the sts, also working K2, K2tog tbl over each cable, so that the number of sts in the cables is halved – the large cables dec to 6 sts and the small cables to 2 sts.

BO all sts on the next row. The sleeve cap measures about 2in/5cm.

Collar

With ndl 7/4.5mm, pick up the sts held around the neck opening – 33 sts from the back neck, 24 sts from each front + 5 extra sts on each side of the back neck + 7 sts on each side of the front neck = 105 sts. Knit 1 edge st, P1, 4 cable sts, P1 for the facing, (P1 + 4 cable sts) 5 times on the neck front, (P1 + 4 cable sts) 8 times on the back neck, (P1, 4 cable sts) 5 times on then neck front, P2, 4 cable sts, P1 and 1 edge st for the facing = a total of 20 small cables. Work the small cables as before until the collar measures 2 3/8–2 3/4in/6–7cm, finishing with a cable crossing row. Purl 1 row on which you BO the 7 facing sts and P2 tog P2 over each cable. BO the last 7 facing sts at the beginning of the next row and purl the rest of the row for the turning. Then work 4 rows in stockinette for the facing and BO.

Buttons

With Trollgarn and crochet hook G/4mm, Ch 4; join into a ring with 1 sl st. Catch the tail end in the ring on the first row so that you don't have to weave it in later – just be sure and pull it tightly to the back later. The back on which you will crochet will become the button's front.

1st rnd: Begin with ch 1, 7 sc in the ring, finish with 1 sl st into the 1st sc.

2nd rnd: *1 sc into 1 st, 2 sc into the next st; repeat from * around.

3rd rnd: *1 sc into each of the next 2 sts, 2 sc in the next st; repeat from * around.

4th and 5th rnds: *1 sc into each of the next 3 sts, 2 sc in the next st; repeat from * around. When the piece is the same diametre as the button, begin decreasing. Dec by: 1 sc in each of the next 3 sts, skip 1 st; repeat from * around and on each rnd until the piece is closed in. However, put the button into the cover after the 2nd dec rnd. Finish by joining with a sl st. Cut yarn, leaving a tail long enough for sewing on the button.

Finishing

Dip and squeeze the body and sleeves in warm water with 1 capful neutral soap per 2.5 gal/10 liters water. Rinse 2–3 times, put the pieces in comforter cover or large nylon washing bag and centrifuge or spin. Lightly spread the pieces to measurement and lay flat to dry. Lightly steam the pieces on the wrong side under a damp cloth. Be extra careful so that the cables are not flattened. Do not press the iron against the pieces but hold it just above so that steam seeps through the cloth and pieces while you cover the work. Steam the seams in the same way on the wrong side. Turn the 7 facing sts along the fronts to the inside and sew them with Hifa 3. Turn in the facing on the collar and sew it to the wrong side.

Make a paper pattern using the collar for measurements. Add 5/8in/1.5cm for a seam allowance and 3/4in/2cm along the lower edge and cut out the velvet. Iron on the interfacing to the velvet and fold in the seam allowance. Sew the velvet lining to the top edge and along the edge st before the cable facing of the front. Cut a 4 3/4in/12cm wide velvet facing which will be enough for the shoulders downward. Iron down about a 3/8in/1cm seam allowance on both

long sides. Sew down the facing, first along the edge st before the cable facing. Form and cut the lining for the neck front; turn in the seam allowance and sew the facing to the collar lining along the neck opening. Finally, sew the inner long side of the facing on the wrong side.

Sew large hooks or small fur hooks on the yoke front so that the front closes edge-to-edge. Sew 3 button loops in the appropriate size for the crocheted buttons on the right front: one at the neck, one at the beginning of the yoke and on centred in between. Sew the crocheted buttons securely to the left front.

Looped bands: The base is crocheted with Trollgarn and the loops with 4 strands of yarn: 1 strand grey mohair, 2 strands black mohair, and 1 strand charcoal grey Hifa 3. All of the looped bands are lined with black velvet. Use the finished pieces for measurements and add a 5/8in/1.5cm seam allowance. Sew the lining on by hand.

Sleeve bands: with Trollgarn and crochet hook H/5mm, ch 63. Beginning in the 2nd ch from hook, work 2 rows of sc working back and forth and cut yarn. Continue with loop crocheting with the 4 strands held together as follows: Wind yarn around the index, middle and ring fingers on the left hand with the yarn crossing on the top side of the index finger.

Insert the crochet hook into the 1st sc (through both loops) and under the cross; pull the cross through the sc. Slip the loop off the fingers. The rest of the sts are crocheted with Hifa 3 – throw one thread onto the hook and draw it through the st on the hook. Crochet 1 loop st in the same way on each sc for

the rest of the row. Arrange the loops so that they lie downwards and out of the way at the end of each row. Turn by ch 1 with 1 strand of Hifa 3 + 1 strand of Trollgarn. Cut the mohair strands + Hifa 3 and make 1 row of sc with Trollgarn. Then, alternately work 1 row of loops with the 4 strands and 1 row sc with Trollgarn until there are 6 loop rows. Finish with 1 row of sc using Trollgarn.

Place the short sides of the sleeve edges together and sew together edge-to-edge, weaving the cut ends of the Trollgarn into the wrong side.

Place the cast-on row for the loop band and the lower edge of the sleeve with right sides facing. Crochet the pieces together with sc using Trollgarn and hook H/5mm.

Lower band: With Trollgarn and hook H/5mm, ch 260. Crochet 6 rows of loops as for the sleeve bands, finishing with 1 row sc with Trollgarn. Place the looped edging right sides facing against the lower edge of the coat. Be sure that the edging is smoothly and evenly placed along the coat's edge; pin. Crochet the pieces together with sc, using Trollgarn and hook H/5mm. The lower edge can also be crocheted in two or more sections and sewn together as were the sleeve bands before they are sewn to the coat.

Detached collar: With Trollgarn and hook H/5.0 m, ch 86. Crochet 12 rows of loops as on the sleeve bands, finishing with 1 row sc and Trollgarn. Sew small fur hooks at the top and bottom of both short sides. Overlap the ends of the collar so they form a V and sew the catches for each hook in the appropriate place.

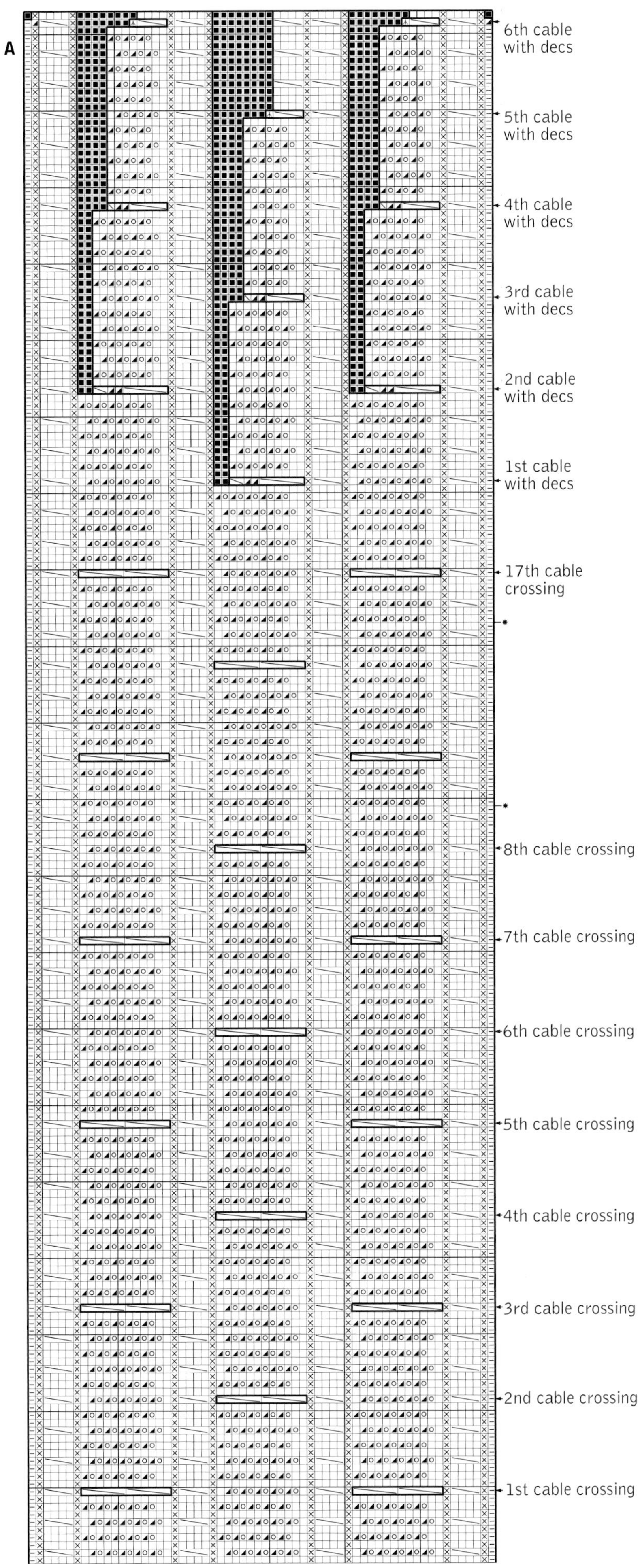

A

6th cable
with decs

5th cable
with decs

4th cable
with decs

3rd cable
with decs

2nd cable
with decs

1st cable
with decs

17th cable
crossing

8th cable crossing

7th cable crossing

6th cable crossing

5th cable crossing

4th cable crossing

3rd cable crossing

2nd cable crossing

1st cable crossing

GRÅSTEIN, POMOR
OG BÅTRYER

GREY STONES,

WHITE SEA TRADING

AND BOAT RUGS

MARGARETHA FINSETH

GREY STONES, WHITE SEA TRADING

AND BOAT RUGS

◣ = K2tog
□ = knit on the right side, purl on the wrong side
⊠ = purl on the right side, knit on the wrong side
⊟ = edge stitch – knit on both right and wrong sides
◉ = yo
◢ = K2tog tbl
◮ = K2tog tbl 2 times and pass 1 st over 2sts = 3 sts decreased
■ = turn in

⬒ = place 2 sts on a cable ndl in front of the work, knit the next
   2 sts tog tbl and then knit the sts from cable ndl

⬓ = place 2 sts on a cable ndl in front of the work, knit the next
   2 sts tog and then knit the sts from cable ndl

▱ = 4 st cable – place 2 sts on a cable ndl in front of the work,
   knit the next 2 sts, then knit sts from cable ndl

▭ = 12 st cable – place 6 sts on a cable ndl in front of the work,
   knit the next 6 sts, then knit sts from cable ndl

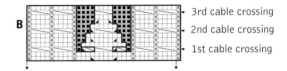

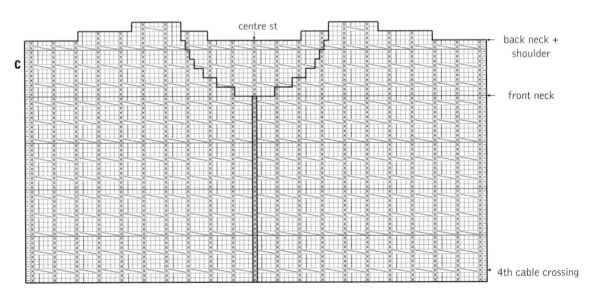

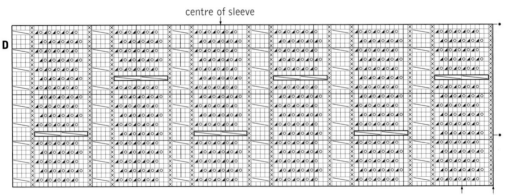

AFTERWORD

The goal of this book has been to produce a colourful, rich, and inspirational book which showcases and documents the variety represented by our knitwear designers. There are those who have taken ideas from our heritage and are the tradition-bearers of Norwegian knitting culture. They show that, what was once handwork and handicraft, is today professional design imbued with high level techniques and creativity, the mastery of which requires solid knowledge and much experience.

Each designer has been totally free to present herself technically and to profile the distinctions of her design form. For that reason, our design book has a wide range of both styles and techniques. You will find patterns with various levels of difficulty, but each has a jumping-off point from which we've determined you can start knitting. However, it cannot be said that all the patterns have an equal level of knitting techniques. Some are dead easy, others require concentration, with attention focussed on the large multicoloured pattern repeats. In some cases the repeats are worked over entire sections of the garment or even over the whole garment. Some designs need experience with and knowledge of finishing techniques, while others will give you plenty of information to go on. Therefore, it is important to judge for yourself which pattern you will be happiest knitting.

Each designer uses her own methods for knitting and finishing in her patterns, and this will vary from designer to designer.